THE
Ultimate
GREETINGS CARD
Book

THE
Ultimate
GREETINGS CARD
Book

CAROLINE GREEN

David & Charles

Acknowledgements and Suppliers

Many thanks for the baby cards originally featured in *Pregnancy and Birth* magazine, and many thanks, also, for the fabric collage and stamped Christmas cards originally featured in *Jane Asher's Christmas Special*, and the work of art cards featured in *Homestyle* magazine.
The following items were supplied by:

Philip and Tacey, North Way, Andover, Hants. SP10 5BA (Tel. 01264 332171) – Pebeo products.

Stamp It for Fun! Catalogue available from 1-9 East Grinstead Road, Lingfield, Surrey RH7 6EP (Tel. 01342 836097) – stamps, embossing powders (various colours and metallic), stamp pads and slow-drying embossing inks.

English Stamp Company, Sunnydown, Worth Matravers, Dorset. BH19 3JP (Tel. 01929 439117) – rubber stamps, inks, rollers, etc.

A DAVID & CHARLES BOOK

First published in the UK in 1996
Reprinted in 1996

Text and artwork Copyright © Caroline Green 1996

Photographs and layout Copyright © David & Charles 1996

Caroline Green has asserted her right to be identified as author of this work in accordance with the Copyright, Designs and Patents Act, 1988.

A catalogue record for this book is available from the British Library.

ISBN 0 7153 0261 2

Photography by Di Lewis

Printed in Great Britain by Butler & Tanner Ltd, Frome

for David & Charles, Brunel House, Newton Abbot, Devon.

Contents

CHAPTER 1

Getting Started

*G*iving a card can bring so much pleasure if you have made it yourself, and yet you don't have to be particularly artistic to create something beautiful and original. Each project can be a way to develop a new craft skill which may grow into a hobby. You may begin by making a single birthday card for a special friend and then find you are inspired to make all this year's Christmas cards.

All the basic techniques are explained here, so it is advisable to read through this chapter first. You will find advice in the instructions for individual cards.

I hope this book will encourage you to try some new skills, and offer the inspiration to help you remember special days with pleasure and a sense of achievement.

Basic equipment for the home-made card-maker

Equipment

All of the equipment shown on pages 6 and 7 is used at some time or another for the projects in this book. The specific materials required for each particular project are listed separately under individual project headings. Some general advice follows for choosing the correct adhesive and card for the job.

ADHESIVES

PVA Glue for paper, card and wood. This glue makes a very strong bond when dry, but because it is water based it may make thinner papers buckle or stretch and wrinkle.

Art and Craft Spray Adhesive (Scotch) for all paper, card and fabric particularly large areas to be glued flat with no risk of wrinkling. It allows for repositioning in the first few minutes.

Hot Glue Gun for gluing heavy items such as shells, buttons or beads to paper and card.

Clear Household Glue (UHU) for gluing card to card and attaching sequins, beads, ribbons, flower stems, etc.

Glue Stick (Pritt Stick) for small paper to paper applications, sealing envelopes and quick repairs.

Using Spray Adhesives
Lay the piece to be glued face down inside an empty cardboard grocery carton. Spray gently, from side to side to give a fairly light even coating. Leave for a few moments and then put it in position on your card. If you have not placed the piece correctly carefully lift it off again and replace within the first few moments. When you are quite happy with it, lay a piece of scrap paper over the top and press it down firmly for a permanent bond.

CARD

Card is available in a wide range of colour shades, but if you can't find exactly what you're looking for, you could extend your choice to plain and printed wrapping papers. To make these strong enough to form a card you will need to bond them on to thin ticket or mounting card using a spray adhesive. For a permanent bond art and craft spray adhesive is ideal, this will glue the pieces together without any risk of buckling or bubbling the surface. Leave the glue to dry thoroughly and always use a very sharp blade before you attempt to cut or score the bonded card or you may damage the thinner paper layer.

Cutting Out Card
For a professional finish accurate cutting is essential. Always use a sharp craft knife, a self-healing cutting mat and a metal ruler. If you don't have a self-healing cutting mat, printed with a grid so that you can cut along the lines for accurate edges, a piece of blockboard and a set square will suffice. The blade of the craft knife will last longer if used with the mat.

Making Envelopes

The size of your finished card is quite important particularly if you want it to fit an existing envelope and then be posted. Tiny cards may well be lost in the post if sent inside a tiny envelope, and extra large ones are equally at risk and may get damaged or bent. If you have an existing envelope you may want to make your card fit into it, or find out the sizes of easily available ready-made ones and make a batch of cards to fit these. This is particularly important when making a series of Christmas cards or invitations.

If the design of the card comes first and it is just a one off-idea for a special occasion, you may feel it warrants making a special envelope in a colour to complement the card, perhaps with a tissue lining to protect a delicate design. You can also incorporate extra stiffening or padding to ensure that the card does not get damaged in transit.

1 Follow the cutting plan (right). The central panel should be slightly larger than your finished card. Carefully lengthen or shorten the flaps so that they fold over and overlap sufficiently in the middle. Make a rough prototype from scrap paper and draw the plan for the finished envelope on to tracing paper.

2 Using a good quality paper, transfer the envelope plan on to it. Cut around the outline using a craft knife, cutting mat and metal ruler. Score along the dotted lines on the right side so that the flaps will bend over neatly to form the envelope.

3 To line the envelope cut out a piece of tissue to the same shape as the envelope, but about 1cm (3/8in) smaller all round. Glue this centrally to the reverse of the envelope.

4 Fold in the two side flaps then glue the lower flap in place to form a pocket for the card. Place the card inside and then run a line of glue along the edge of the upper flap. Fold this over and press to seal.

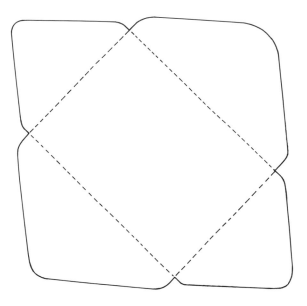

Use this basic plan to make your own rough prototype before cutting out an envelope. Adjust the proportions to match your chosen card

Making Mounts

The mount you choose is an important part of the structure of your greetings card. It should complement both the colours and style of the the design, and the material you choose to make your mount should be physically strong enough to stand up.

There are two main types of mount to consider. The simplest is a plain mount where the picture, flower or embroidered design is attached to the front of a folded piece of decorative paper or card. The other type is a window mount, usually made of medium-thick card, which has an opening or 'window' cut in

the centre. This can be used as it is or covered with fabric or paper. The window can be decorated with ruled borders drawn with a silver or gold felt-tipped pen, or a colour chosen to match the design which it frames.

Shaped window mounts also create lovely cards with the design of the window itself forming part of the main motif.

To make a mount for your card you will need an assortment of materials including: assorted papers and fabric; marbled paper or giftwrap; white paper; coloured card; silver or gold felt-tipped pens; ribbon.

PLAIN MOUNT

Choose decorative or plain card that will go with your design to form the actual card. Your cut-out design can be glued, stitched or tied in place in a simple or highly decorative way. If you have a very small motif a hand-torn undermount, positioned behind the motif, can emphasise and make the most of it.

1 Decide on the size of your finished card and cut out a piece of thin card measuring roughly the height your card will be, and twice its width. Lay a metal ruler across the middle of the card on the right side and score a vertical line using

Specially-made envelopes will complement your original card designs. You can even use patterned giftwrap if you glue a plain label on the front for the address

the back of a knife blade or a worn out ball-point pen. This should make a sharp indentation in the surface of the card but will not cut it.

2 You will find that you can now bend the card easily. Fold it in half and turn it over to the back then sharpen the fold by rolling it with a wallpaper seam roller, or a similar tool.

3 Now use the grid lines on your mat, or a set square, to mark the top, bottom and side edges of the folded card so that it is exactly square. Cut through both layers together using a sharp craft knife and a metal ruler so that the back and front match exactly.

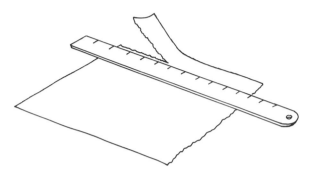

4 For a smaller undermount you can add a piece of paper with hand-torn edges. Cut the paper about 2.5cm (1in) larger than you want the finished piece to be. Place it on a flat surface and lay a metal ruler on top, a little way in from one edge. Hold the ruler down firmly with one hand and tear the free edge of the paper along the ruler to leave a deckle-edged effect like hand-made paper. Turn the paper around and tear the other edges in the same way. This works very well with good quality pastel and watercolour papers. Use spray glue to fix the undermount to the front of the card.

5 Try making two and three fold cards for different effects (see illustration below).

6 For a more luxurious look, you can make a lining from white paper on which you can stamp or write your message. Cut a piece of white paper slightly smaller than the unfolded card. Fold it in half and glue lightly to the inside of the card near the fold.

WINDOW MOUNTS

Window mounts are ideal for displaying embroideries and designs which use fabrics. They require a little more care in the cutting but it is quite easy to achieve a professional result. You can buy ready-made cards like this in many different designs, sizes and colours but you will find that making your own is cheaper and much more flexible.

1 Cut the card roughly to size, making it three times the width of the front of the finished card, and score two folds to make three equal panels. Mark the area for the window on the centre panel, in pencil. If the window is to be square or rectangular, lay a ruler along one side of the window-shape and run the knife along it so that it cuts just outside the line. Repeat this on the other three sides and lift out the centre piece. Now try the mount over your design.

2 Mark on any border lines in pencil. Use silver or gold felt-tipped pens to draw these in varying widths. You may also like to add strips of marbled paper or giftwrap to further embellish the mount. If so, cut one strip for each side and glue them in place mitring the corners neatly (see page 12).

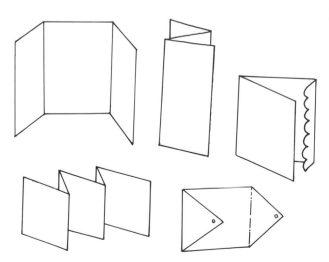

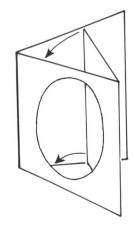

3 You can also cut out round and oval windows for different projects. Use upturned bowls, cups or glasses to mark out the shapes accurately. Several small rectangles set together will look like a real window and you can decorate the outside of the card with pretend curtains and the inside of the right-hand flap with a lovely view.

4 To enclose an embroidery design completely and make the inside of the card really neat a window mount is ideal. The two folds in the card create three panels, and if you position your design on the inside of the right-hand panel it will appear in the window. Spray the inside of the central panel with glue and fold the right-hand panel into place behind it.

Borders

Window mounts can be decorated with ruled, paper or fabric borders for a truly professional finish.

Ruled Borders A frame of hand-ruled lines in gold or silver can give a modern or traditional look to your design.

1 Mark out borders around your window or undermount with light pencil lines. Using a ruler measure the distance around the window or the edge of the undermount.

2 Lay the ruler along one line with the bevel underneath. This ensures that the edge of the ruler is not touching the design.

3 When using a gold or silver felt-tipped pen shake as directed to distribute the colour evenly and then test it on a scrap of paper to produce a smooth, even line. Draw the border line following the edge of the ruler and leave to dry off.

4 Turn the card round and draw the border line on the other sides in the same way.

5 If you are making a double or even a triple border, complete the inside one first, then work outwards in the same way for the other lines.

Paper Borders Decorative strips of paper make interesting borders and will flatter some of the more simple designs. The corners of the strips should be mitred and an easy way of doing this is described below.

1 To make the decorative border, cut four strips of paper a suitable width to go around your design or window. Cut the pieces longer than the sides of the window to allow for making mitred corners.

2 Spray the reverse side of the strips with adhesive and then place them lightly around the window making sure the inner edge of each strip is the same distance from the edge of the window. The adhesive will allow you to reposition the strips for accuracy.

3 Lay a ruler across each corner in turn, lining up the edge of it with the inner and outer points where the strips overlap. Use a craft knife to carefully cut the mitres at each corner going through both thicknesses of paper at the same time to make a perfect join. Remove the excess pieces of paper and press the strips down firmly to bond.

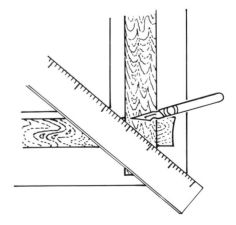

Personalised Message

Many people can make a delightful design for a card but tend to panic at the thought of doing any lettering. If you prefer, you can write your personal message inside the card in your own handwriting but for a professional look you could choose another method for the lettering on the front of the card.

CALLIGRAPHY

You can use decorative lettering in wonderful colours and arrangements for both the front and the inside of your card. There are many inexpensive italic pens on the market, both fountain and felt-tipped, with instruction books that should help you to produce most acceptable writing.

STAMPS

There are several companies marketing rubber stamps for home craft use and some of these have messages as part of the design. You can use these to print the wording inside your greetings cards, or make some of the more decorative versions into the main design on the front of the card. The inks used with these stamps vary from quick-drying coloured inks to metallic-embossed inks for a very professional and expensive-looking finish.

PHOTOCOPYING

Photocopy lettering from newspapers, magazines and old greetings cards and then cut them out or trace them to use on your cards. Enlarged numbers are particularly useful for special birthdays and anniversaries while letters are good for names and linked initials on wedding or engagement cards.

COMPUTER PRINTING

If you are lucky enough to own a computer and printer you will be able to print virtually any message. Work on white paper and make this into a card lining to glue inside your finished card. Or you could cut out larger lettering and glue other motifs around the words to make a most attractive and personal design.

STENCIL LETTERING

Plastic stencils have been around for many years and they can be used very easily and cheaply for making cards. The secret of a good finish is to draw a faint pencil line before you begin and then line up the base of all the letters along this. It is also a good plan to do a rough version on scrap paper to adjust spacing and to determine the best position for each word or number. Fine felt-tipped pens and coloured pencils are the easiest things to use or you could draw the outlines with a technical drawing pen and colour in the centre of each letter with watercolour or poster paints.

You could also cut out your own letters or words in stencil film and paint with a brush or sponge using acrylic paints.

DRY TRANSFER LETTERING

There are several makes available from art and graphic suppliers. They come in sheets of individual letters which you arrange along a guide line to form the words. The letters are made from very thin, self-adhesive plastic sheets which you transfer by burnishing with a ball-point pen on to paper. It is quite expensive to buy but there is a very large range of sizes and typefaces so you can achieve exactly the right finish. It would be ideal as a way of making a master copy for an invitation which you could photocopy as many times as necessary and then mount and hand colour. It is also perfect for making the number cards described on page 18.

If you haven't got time to create your wording from single letters, you can also buy sheets of ready spaced messages such as Happy Birthday, Best Wishes and Merry Christmas which are much easier to use as you do not need to arrange the letters individually.

Displaying Cards

Displaying cards in large quantities, especially at Christmas time, can be an art in itself. Here are several ideas for useful and decorative displays.

CARD HOLDER

This is made from two sheets of medium-thick card held together in the centre and hung on the wall. The greetings cards are then pushed between the card layers at various angles for display. The holder can be made in a long shape to hold the greetings cards in a vertical display or you could make it round or star shaped and display the cards in a circle.

To make a card holder you will need: medium-thick card; self-adhesive plate hanger; tartan ribbon.

The wall holder, ribbon bow display and simple stand show how with a little ingenuity you can display your finished cards in a variety of ways

1 For the front of the card holder cut out two stars from silver or gold card and a zig-zag edged rectangle of tartan patterned card. (You may need to mount tartan-patterned paper on to card to achieve the right thickness.)

2 From the medium-thick card, cut the back a little larger than the front piece. Keep to a simple rectangular shape as this will not be seen when the cards are in position.

3 Spread PVA glue down the centre of the backing piece and place the front piece centrally in position. Weight it down with heavy books and leave the glue to dry hard.

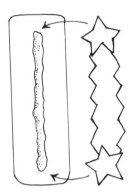

4 Turn the holder over and glue the plate hanger to the back so that the ring is at the top for hanging. You can also decorate the front of the holder with ribbon or seasonal decorations.

5 To display the cards, push them between the layers of card all round the holder. You can either aim for a random arrangement or a regular one depending on your taste and the cards you have.

RIBBON AND BOW DISPLAY

For a pretty wall-mounted display, wide satin or florist's ribbon makes an ideal surface on which to glue or staple cards. You can also add the same or contrasting bows at the top and bottom to make a special feature.

1 Cut a piece of ribbon at least 1m (1yd) long. Tie some of the same or contrasting ribbon into a large bow and glue this to the top of the ribbon so that the tails of the bow hang down either side.

2 Staple or stick the greetings cards to the length of ribbon starting just under the bow and working your way down to the end. Leave a small gap between each card so that you can see the flat ribbon passing behind them.

3 To finish off, leave about 5cm (2in) of ribbon free at the end and make another bow as for the top. Glue this in place and trim the bow tails to complete.

4 Hang this on the wall using a picture hook or sticky pads for a less permanent effect.

SIMPLE STAND

This tiny stand is very useful if you want to display a single card for some time. The lower edge of the greetings card is held between two pieces of wooden beading or moulding mounted on to a piece of card. You can paint the stand for a more decorative effect. To make a simple stand you will need: wooden moulding or quarter-round beading; small hacksaw; fine sandpaper; PVA wood glue; a piece of thick card; acrylic paint; watercolour brushes.

1 Using the saw, cut two pieces about 10cm (4in) long. Sand the cut edges until smooth and glue them centrally on to the piece of thick card, leaving a small gap between them to slot the card in place.

2 Leave the glue to dry then trim the card base to the desired shape to support the stand when the greetings card is in position. The larger the greetings card the larger the base of the stand will need to be.

3 Paint the stand in the desired colour and leave to dry before use.

CHAPTER 2

Birthday Cards

*I*t is not always easy to find exactly
the right card for a particular friend
or family member, but what could be
more personal than a card made for a
special birthday? Not only will these
cards be treasured but they are great
fun to make and certainly make a
welcome change from the run-of-the mill
ready-made cards.

*Choose the perfect card for the perfect occasion.
Any of these designs can be adapted to make
greetings cards for friends or family of all ages*

NUMBER CARDS

Choose one of these designs and then add the numbers to correspond with the recipient's birthday. If you do not feel confident to draw the number you require, look through magazines and books to find the style you want, and trace the number from there. Dry transfer lettering is also a useful alternative.

MATERIALS
Gold paper or thin card
Folded cards (see page 11) in plain, patterned or metallic card
Scraps of hand-made paper in subtle tones
Gold felt-tipped pen
Pebeo gold and black relief outliners
Pebeo gutta in pearl colours to go with your card

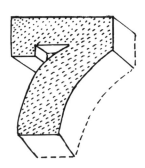

1 Draw or trace off the appropriate numbers and transfer the shape to gold paper or thin card. Then cut out carefully using a craft knife and cutting mat.

2 Spray the reverse side of the numbers with glue and place on your prepared card. Add cut-out motifs and decorations made with the gold outliner and felt-tipped pen.

3 For the card featuring the large number enlarge the appropriate number from a newspaper or magazine and then add the shaded areas. To do this, draw angled lines from all the points on the right hand side of the figure. Then join up these points following the shape of the edge of the number.

4 Transfer this design on to the front of your folded card and then draw the outlines with a black outliner. Make random patterns in black in the shaded areas and then decorate the main area of the figure with the other pearly colours of gutta. Draw zig-zags, dots, lines and curves in all the colours to fill the area with pattern.

5 For the key card, trace and cut out the key shape below using the thin gold card. You can add the numbers into the top of the key, as here, or leave it as an empty hole.

6 Thread a ready-made tassel into the top of the key and then glue the key at an angle on to a plain card mount, in the colour of your choice.

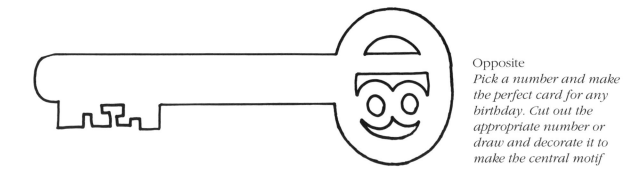

Opposite
Pick a number and make the perfect card for any birthday. Cut out the appropriate number or draw and decorate it to make the central motif

FOR FAMILY AND FRIENDS

In order to get just the right card for everyone the best plan is to make your own. You can be as artistic as you like, and hopefully the designs in this section will inspire you to try your hand at something totally new.

Cut-out Cards

These cards leave you in no doubt as to who they are for. The lettering is simple and joined into one block to make a stylish statement.

MATERIALS
Silver or gold card
Red or silver hologram card

1 Fold your card and cut it roughly to size. Select lettering from newspapers, magazines or old greetings cards, and reduce or enlarge to the required size. Cut the letters out, arrange into words, and trace them on to the front of the card ready for cutting out (the fold should line up with the left-hand edge or the top of the row of letters). Draw over the outline of the letters with a hard pencil to leave an indented line in the surface of the foil to follow when cutting.

2 Using a sharp craft knife and cutting mat, cut through both layers of card at once. Cut out all the internal holes first while the card is at its strongest. Use a metal ruler as a guide when cutting the straight lines. Make sure that the letters are connected as they are cut out; if each one is not joined to its neighbour they will fall apart when cut.

3 Carefully cut out all the various notches and shapes along the edge to complete the card. Write the message inside, following the shapes of the cut out letters.

Sun Card

Bring a little sunshine into the life of someone special. This card can be seen in the photograph on page 16.

MATERIALS
Picture of sun cut from a magazine or giftwrap
Shiny black plain card mount
Pebeo gold relief outliner
Coloured folded paper for lining

1 Cut out your sun motif then cut a round window in a plain card mount. Make sure the window is slightly larger than the sun motif.

2 Glue the sun to the lining sheet to fit behind the window and decorate around the edge with tiny dots made with the gold outliner. Leave to dry. Using the gold outliner, decorate around the edge of the window with squiggly lines and dots to look like the sun's rays. When all the gold is dry, glue the lining inside the card to complete.

A steady hand and a sharp knife are two most important things when making these sparkling cut-out cards

Tree of Life

This silk painted tree of life design would make a perfect card for a special birthday such as an eighteenth or twenty-first, or even a twelfth (silk) wedding anniversary card. The tree is a wonderfully optimistic symbol of life, ideal for a special occasion

MATERIALS
Fine white silk (about 22cm (8¹/₂in) square)
Pebeo silk paints in red, yellow and blue
Tubes of Pebeo gutta in pearly blue and gold
Watercolour brushes
Watercolour paint palette
Fine black waterproof felt-tipped pen
Adjustable frame for stretching the silk

1 Using the black felt-tipped pen, trace the design directly off the card opposite, this is exactly the right size for the final card. Follow the silk painting instructions on page 98.

2 Draw the border and the leaves using the blue gutta, and the tree trunk and the fruit with the gold gutta. Leave to set for an hour or two,

3 Mix up the colours in the palette and paint in your design. Leave it to dry then fix the silk paints by ironing on the reverse side, following the maker's instructions carefully.

4 Tape your finished silk painting inside a window mount with a rectangular window cut in the centre section. Fold over and glue the end section to neaten the inside of the card.

Dancing Teddies

The dancing teddies pictured on page 17 are ideal for younger members of the family. They can be used individually as a fun card or made together in a row to form a frieze for a child's room. You could make your card so that there is a teddy to celebrate each year.

MATERIALS
Silver felt-tipped pen
Buff-coloured lightweight card
Scrap of narrow ribbon

1 Cut a piece of buff-coloured card and fold it vertically in a concertina fashion to make as many teddies as you need. If you want to make more than about five teddies it is best to do them in two lots to avoid the risk of the paper layers slipping as you cut.

2 Trace out the teddy shape on the right. Tape the tracing on to the top of the folded card so that the paws overlap the folded edges slightly.

3 Using a sharp knife, cut out around the edge of the teddy making sure that the paws stay joined at the folds.

4 Open out the card and draw the features on to each bear with the silver pen and then write on your message. Add a tiny ribbon bow to the front teddy to dress him up.

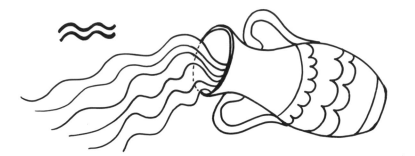

AQUARIUS (21 January–19 February)
element **air**
colour **turquoise**
stone **aquamarine**

TAURUS (21 April–22 May)
element **earth**
colour **pink**
stone **sapphire**

PISCES (20 February–20 March)
element **water**
colour **sea green**
stone **moonstone**

GEMINI (23 May–21 June)
element **air**
colour **yellow**
stone **emerald**

ARIES (21 March–20 April)
element **fire**
colour **red**
stone **diamond**

CANCER (22 June–22 July)
element **water**
colour **silver-grey**
stone **pearl**

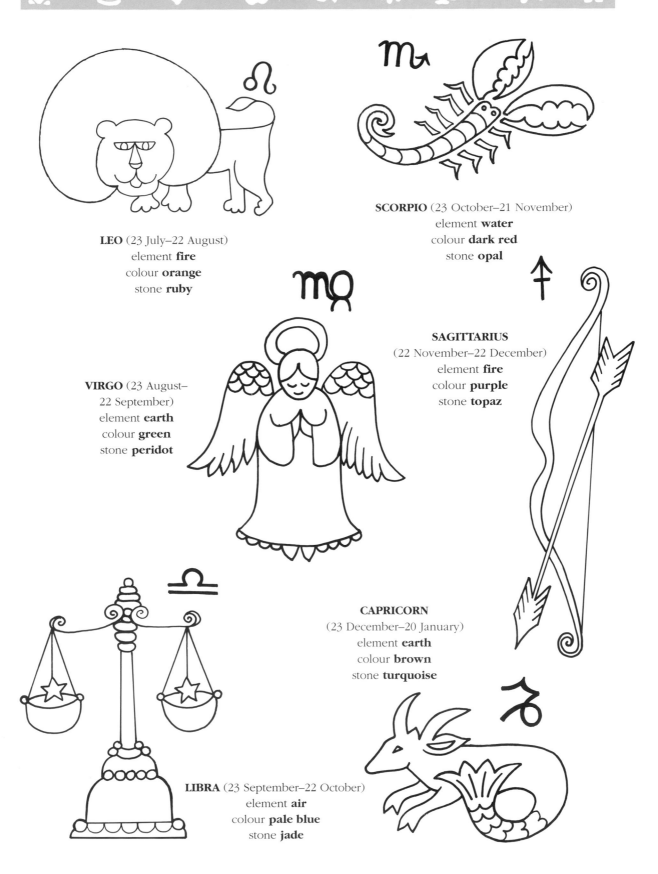

LEO (23 July–22 August)
element **fire**
colour **orange**
stone **ruby**

SCORPIO (23 October–21 November)
element **water**
colour **dark red**
stone **opal**

VIRGO (23 August–
22 September)
element **earth**
colour **green**
stone **peridot**

SAGITTARIUS
(22 November–22 December)
element **fire**
colour **purple**
stone **topaz**

CAPRICORN
(23 December–20 January)
element **earth**
colour **brown**
stone **turquoise**

LIBRA (23 September–22 October)
element **air**
colour **pale blue**
stone **jade**

CHAPTER 3

Celebration Cards

*H*ere is a host of ideas for special celebration cards which will delight anyone lucky enough to receive one. You can celebrate Christmas, Thanksgiving, New Year, Valentine's Day, St Patrick's Day and many more in your own unique style. Picture your card on the mantelpiece of a friend and plan your design accordingly.

Using a stencilling or stamping technique is the ideal way of making a quantity of cards and gives a very professional result. A greetings message stamp is perfect for the lettering inside the card; you can stamp this directly on to the inside flap or make a white lining sheet to fit inside.

There are many festivals and celebrations throughout the world. Here are card ideas to help you celebrate a few of them

CHRISTMAS

Making your own Christmas cards is great fun, less expensive, and far more personal than sending out the ready-made type. Stencilling and stamping techniques are the ideal ways of making a quantity of Christmas cards and will give a very professional result. A greetings message stamp is perfect for wording inside the card.

Silver Tree Card

This cut-out collage pictured opposite can be made with any pieces of left-over material that you already have. The silver mirror card creates a stunning effect and brings the fabric scraps to life with a little Christmas magic.

MATERIALS
Scraps of brightly coloured fabric
Silver mirror card

1 Trace off the half pattern of the Christmas tree on page 127 on to folded tracing paper, placing the fold along dotted line. Turn the paper over and trace in the other half to make the complete shape.

2 Transfer this to the reverse side of a piece of the silver card, positioning it so that it will be on the front of the card when the mount is folded.

3 Using a craft knife and cutting mat, cut out the Christmas tree. Score a vertical line 1cm (³⁄₈in) away from the left-hand edge of the tree on the silver side of the card. Fold in half and trim the other three edges to form the card.

4 Cut a piece of coloured card the same size as the folded greetings card. Slip this inside and draw the position of the tree, baubles and pot in pencil. Cut out scraps of various fabrics, slightly larger than these shapes and look at them through the front of the cut out card. When you are happy with the arrangement, glue them in place to the coloured card.

5 Open the greetings card and spread glue over the inside of the front flap. Press the coloured card in place so that you can see the fabric correctly positioned through the holes.

Star of Gold

A simple star can look both rich and festive when you use different textures of gold.

MATERIALS
Gold fabric or shiny card
Textured gold card
Pebeo gold relief outliner

1 Using the star template on page 127 as your guide trace off the shape and cut it out from a piece of gold fabric or shiny gold card to make the central motif.

2 Make up a small square plain mount from the gold textured card.

3 Use spray adhesive to glue the star to the centre of the card mount.

4 Finally, using the gold relief outliner, draw a line just outside the edge of the star following the shape carefully.

The same cut-out collage techniques pictured below can be used with other shapes too. A simple star cut out of dark blue card with scraps of satin would look very dramatic. Holly leaves and berries would also work well, perhaps with patterned card and plain fabrics

Hark the Herald Angels

You can make many cards like this from a single sheet of Christmas giftwrap. Tear or carefully cut around motifs and mount on card, adding tiny stars at the corners, drawn with gold relief outliner, for decoration.

MATERIALS
Giftwrap with Christmas motifs
Folded cards in silver or blue
Gold cake frill
Pebeo gold relief outliner

1 Using a small pair of scissors, carefully cut out your chosen motif from the giftwrap. You may need to use a craft knife and cutting mat to remove any areas of the background pattern which appear in the centre of the motif.

2 Spray the reverse of the motif with glue and position it on the front of your folded card.

3 Cut the edge from the gold cake frill and glue pieces round the motif to make a frame. Overlap at the corners and then cut through to make a mitre (see page 12).

4 For the hand-torn edged cards, cut out the motif leaving more background than you need then use a metal ruler to tear the edges into a square around it (see page 11). Tear off the corners in the same way and then use spray adhesive to glue it to the front of your folded card.

5 Decorate the corners of the finished card with little stars drawn with the gold outliner.

Silk-painted Christmas Star

A gorgeous Christmas design in an unusual blue and yellow colour theme (see photograph on page 36). For a more detailed explanation of the silk painting technique, see page 98.

MATERIALS
Fine black waterproof felt-tipped pen
Adjustable frame for stretching the silk
Fine white silk (about 18cm (7in) square)
Pebeo silk paints in red, yellow and blue
Pebeo thinner
Tubes of Pebeo gutta in silver and gold
Watercolour brushes
Watercolour paint palette

1 Using the black felt-tipped pen trace the design carefully from the card shown same size on page 36. Cut out the silk slightly larger than the outer edge of the design. Using the frame, stretch the silk. Tape the design underneath the silk, so that you can see it clearly.

2 Using the tube of silver gutta draw the main parts of the design. Then draw the inner stars and the dots with the gold gutta. Leave to set for an hour or two before you begin painting.

3 Mix up the colours for the design in the palette and paint in your design. To make a slightly warmer yellow, add a drop of red to the yellow silk paint.

4 Leave the finished design to dry, then fix the silk paints by ironing on the reverse side of the fabric, following the maker's instructions.

5 Tape your finished silk painting inside a window mount with a rectangular window cut in the centre section. Fold over and glue the end

Opposite This luxurious selection of Christmas cards features three Hark the Herald Angels cards and the Star of Gold (page 32)

section to neaten the inside of the card. Draw stars and circles as a border round the edge of the window using a silver felt-tipped pen.

This silk-painted Christmas star is printed the same size as the finished design and can therefore be used as a template for tracing off

NEW YEAR

There are many New Year festivals and celebrations throughout the world. If you have friends who celebrate a different New Year to your own why not find out a little more about it and choose some of the special motifs or designs to make a greetings card especially for them.

Divali, Hindu New Year

Divali is the Hindu festival of light which marks the beginning of the new year. It is a moveable feast that is celebrated at the end of October or at the beginning of November.

MATERIALS
Red card
Gold card
Scraps of paper to cut out the candle and flame

1 Using the red card, prepare a plain mount measuring 14.5 x 21cm (5¾ x 8in) by following the instructions given on page 10, in the first chapter.

2 Trace off the outline on the right, reversing your tracing paper (as described on page 32) for the other half, and transfer this to the inside of the front flap of your card mount. Using a craft knife and cutting mat, cut out the shaded areas.

3 Place the piece of gold card behind the cut out area and trim to size around the edge. Spray the inside of the front flap with glue and then mount the gold card in place to show through the cut out pattern.

4 Cut out the candle and flame from pieces of coloured paper and use the spray adhesive to mount the shapes on to the gold card inside the arch shape. Choose colours appropriate to the festival of light; in the example pictured on page 38 the candle flame has been cut from small scraps of shiny hologram paper, giving it a shimmering quality.

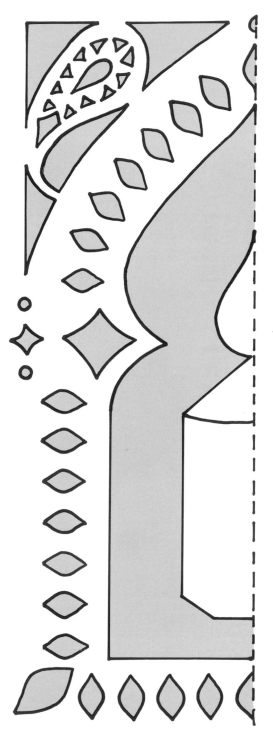

Sparkling gold and cheerful red is the theme for these New Year celebration cards, bringing good luck wishes for the future

Universal New Year

Ring in the New Year in any language with this elegant clock set at just after midnight with the bells tolling for joy.

MATERIALS
Plain red card mount
Gold marbled paper
Gold mirror card and white card scraps

1 Trace off the templates for the hands, bells and clock, turning the tracing paper over to draw the other half of the clock. Transfer the traced-off shapes to the appropriate coloured card. You will need two bells. Cut out the outlines.

2 Spray the backs of these pieces with glue. First, mount the clock centrally onto the front of the red card. Then put on the face, setting the hands just after midnight, and lastly place the bells in the top corners.

Rosh Hashanah, Jewish New Year

This card could also be used to celebrate Chanukah, the Jewish festival of light, which is close to Christmas.

MATERIALS
Tiny gold beads
Red plain card mount
Gold marbled paper
Pebeo gold relief outliner

1 Fold a piece of tracing paper in half and, place the fold on the dotted line of the candelabra template on the next page. Trace off the pattern, then turn the paper over and trace in the other half to make the complete shape. Note that the tiny slave candle in the centre should only appear on one half of your design. Transfer your candelabra outline on to the gold marbled paper

2 Use the gold outliner to draw over the traced lines filling in some areas and leaving others as outlines.

3 Draw the flames of the candles last and while the outliner is still wet, press a tiny gold bead into each flame to give it a sparkle of light. Leave to dry then trim the paper with the hand-torn method descibed on page 11, and glue it to the front of your folded red card.

Use the template on the right to make the card for Rosh Hashanah, and the one below for the Chinese New Year

Chinese New Year

The beautiful Chinese lettering is cut in gold and mounted on traditional red for good luck.

MATERIALS
Shiny gold card
Shiny red plain card mount

1 Use a photocopier to enlarge the Chinese lettering above. Trace off the design before transferring the shapes to the gold card. Then cut them out carefully using a craft knife and cutting mat.

2 Fold the shiny red card to make a plain mount. Then spray the back of the gold cut-out lettering with adhesive and position it on the front of the card making sure it is the correct way up.

RELIGIOUS THEMES

The stained-glass technique described below is perfect for greetings cards with a religious theme. The design is drawn on to acetate sheet using black outliner to represent the leading and then the special glass paints are flooded into each area.

MATERIALS
Acetate sheet
Pebeo black outliner
Pebeo glass paints in red, blue and yellow
Watercolour brushes
Shiny silver card
White scrap paper
Plain card mount

1 Trace off the designs below and use coloured pencils to roughly indicate the colours you intend to use in each area. Then tape a piece of the acetate sheet over the tracing.

2 Lay the pieces on to white scrap paper so that you can see the lines really clearly. Using the black outliner, follow the lines carefully, trying to make them as even as possible. Take care not to smudge the lines as you work. Leave to dry for about an hour.

3 When the outliner is quite dry use the glass paints to fill in each area with colour. Dip the watercolour brush into the paint and then work it quickly over the acetate between the black

The crucifix template on the left is suitable for Christening, Easter and Confirmation cards; and the Star of David template below could be used for a variety of religious occasions, particularly Barmitzvah

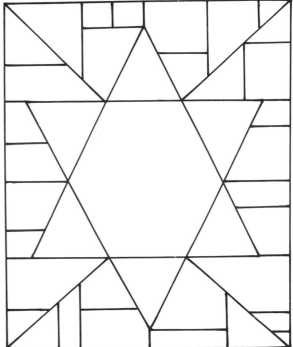

lines. Work on one area at a time and use plenty of paint to give a smooth finish. Do not use too many brush strokes or you will create bubbles that may spoil the surface texture of the paint. The colours are fully mixable so you can experiment with creating as many different shades as you wish.

4 Leave the paint until it is completely dry and then mount it on to shiny silver card so that the colours show up well. Use narrow strips of masking tape to hold it in place.

5 Cut a window in the front flap of a plain card mount and glue the stained glass panel behind it. The window should be slightly smaller than the painted area of the acetate to hide the edges and the tape.

Choose this dramatic stained-glass technique to make cards for Easter, Confirmation, Barmitzvah or Christenings. A black outliner is used to represent the leading and the rich glass colours are added for stunning effect

VALENTINE AND ANNIVERSARIES

Special cards to send to a loved one or to your parents on an anniversary are always welcome especially when they are hand made. Choose a simple heart shape and be as creative as possible when you decorate it.

Hand-drawn Heart

This quick hand-drawn design (pictured on page 45) is charmingly simple.

MATERIALS
Red plain card mount
Brown block printing ink
A small sheet of glass
White spirit
A rubber roller
Red felt-tipped pen

1 Following the instructions for mono-printing on page 59, roll some of the printing ink on to a sheet of glass and lay the paper face down on to the paint. Now draw on your design using a ball point pen or a sharp pencil.

2 When the drawing is complete lift the paper off and leave the print to dry. Colour in the centre of the heart with the red felt-tipped pen and then cut out the paper around the design using pinking shears.

3 Spray the reverse of the design with adhesive and then position it centrally on to the coloured card mount.

Homespun Valentine

For a really quick Valentine card with a homespun look, mount a heart design cut from giftwrap on to white card and finish with some simple stitching.

MATERIALS
Heart design cut from giftwrap or magazine
Two pieces of white card
White embroidery cotton
Large needle

1 Cut out the heart motif and background, and use spray glue to mount it on to some white card.

2 Cut this out to form a rectangle and trim the other piece of card to match.

3 Punch small holes all round the edge of the card front and matching holes on the left-hand edge of the card back. The holes should be about 1cm (³/8in) apart.

4 Thread the needle with the white cotton and blanket stitch (see diagram overleaf) all round the card using the punched holes. Tie the cotton neatly to the lower left-hand corner and work from left to right. When you reach a corner,

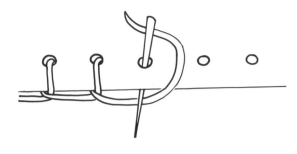

stitch into the corner hole three times to negotiate the pointed edge of the card neatly.

5 When you reach the top left-hand corner, line up the back piece of the card and stitch the last side through both layers to form the hinge of the card. Finish the stitches by tying the thread neatly at the back.

Padded Heart

A scrap of beautiful silk was the inspiration for the padded card shown opposite. The fabric is glued over a little wadding and then surrounded with a heart-shaped mount. Choose stiff card so that the fabric is held in position.

MATERIALS
Stiff plain card mount about 13cm (5in) square
Stiff pink card
Scrap of pink shot silk
Scraps of polyester wadding
Pebeo bronze gutta

1 Using the smallest heart template on page 126 draw a window on to the stiff pink card. Use a pair of compasses to draw a slightly larger circle around this. Then cut out the circle and the heart shape with a craft knife.

2 Place this circle centrally on to the front of the folded mount and draw round the inside and

outside edges lightly with a pencil to mark the position of the wadding and fabric.

3 Spread a thin layer of glue over the heart outline on the front of the card. Tear the wadding into scraps and place on the glue. Lay the fabric over the top and glue the raw edges to the card. Make sure the fabric does not go outside the edge of the circle.

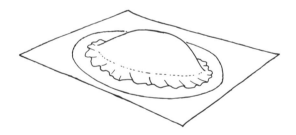

4 Spread glue over the back of the card circle and place it over the fabric. Press it down all

Use this list of wedding anniversaries to inspire you to make the perfect card for your loved ones

1st	Paper	*	7th	Wool	*	13th	Lace	*	35th	Coral
2nd	Cotton	*	8th	Salt	*	14th	Ivory	*	40th	Ruby
3rd	Leather	*	9th	Copper	*	15th	Crystal	*	45th	Sapphire
4th	Fruit and flowers	*	10th	Tin	*	20th	China	*	50th	Gold
5th	Wood	*	11th	Steel	*	25th	Silver	*	55th	Emerald
6th	Sugar and cakes	*	12th	Silk and linen	*	30th	Pearl	*	60th	Diamond

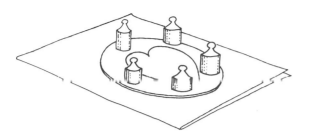

5 When the glue has dried decorate the edge of the circle with tiny dots of bronze gutta.

round so that the padded fabric pushes through the heart-shaped hole. Leave to dry with the circle weighted down all round.

Many different techniques can be used to make up a Valentine card for the one you love. With traditional red hearts or red backgrounds the hand-drawn (above) and homespun (below) Valentines have a charm all of their own. The soft pink padded heart on a cream background (middle) makes a subtle, feminine-looking card

A DATE TO REMEMBER

All through the year there are special festivals and holidays which call for special cards. St Patrick's Day and the Fourth of July are just a couple of the days to celebrate with a creative greeting.

Fourth of July

Choose the famous stars and stripes to make a card that suggests both flags and fireworks.

MATERIALS
Shiny red card
Scraps of blue, white and shiny gold card
Self adhesive gold stars
Gold extra fine marker pen

1 Cut out a piece of the red card to measure 12.5 x 29.5cm (5 x 11¾in). Score the card twice on the right side from one long edge to the other then fold the flaps in to meet in the centre.

2 Cut strips of white card 18mm (¹¹⁄₁₆in) wide. Using spray adhesive, glue to the front of the card to make even red and white stripes.

3 Trace off the starburst design, cut it out in blue card and draw the lines in gold. Cut a star from shiny gold card and glue it to the starburst.

4 Glue the starburst to the right hand flap of the card so the points of the star hold the card closed. Add gold stars following the photograph.

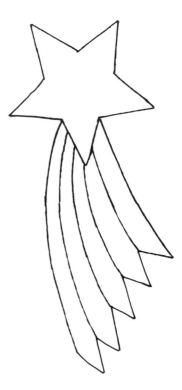

St Patrick's Day

The Irish shamrock cards, made to celebrate St Patrick's Day, can be seen on pages 30 and 31.

MATERIALS
Green card
Gold or silver extra fine marker pen

1 Trace the shamrock pattern on page 126 onto tracing paper and use this to cut a shamrock template in scrap card. Lay this on the green card and draw several shamrocks with a sharp pencil. Cut out the shamrocks with a craft knife. Arrange them in pairs for each card.

Celebrate Independence Day on Fourth of July with dramatic stars and stripes in red, white and blue. The starburst is designed to hold the flaps of the card together

2 Cut from the top to the centre point on one shamrock and from the base to the centre point on the other one. Slot the two pieces together and trim the base if necessary to enable the card to stand up.

3 Unslot the two shamrocks and use the marker pen to decorate them. Draw a wiggly line all over one side of one to make an interesting and random textured pattern. On the other side write a message for St Patrick's Day. Finally, slot the two shamrocks together.

Printed Cards

*G*et into mass production with the
following variety of printing
techniques which include using a simple
potato cut, stamping and stencilling
and a few others besides. Any occasion
that needs lots of cards sent out will be
perfect for this treatment. Featured in
this chapter are inspirational designs
for weddings, birth announcements,
Christmas cards, invitations and house-
moving cards.

*Experiment with stencils, stamping and
embossing, potato prints and lino cuts to make
some unique cards of your own*

POTATO CUTS

Cut your raised shape into the halved potato. Place on a kitchen towel or something similar to soak up any excess liquid. Make sure the design is completely flat or it will not print evenly.

Moving House Card

Send out details of your new address using a quick and easy potato cut featuring a house design. Two are provided here. Use one or both, as you choose, to create a picture. To save on envelopes, you can stamp your chosen design directly on to a postcard (opposite).

MATERIALS
Large potato
Large and small kitchen knives
Watercolour brushes
Acrylic or poster paints in red and blue
White card
Printed name and address

1 Cut the potato in half with the large knife to give a smooth, flat surface. Leave the cut edges of the potato to stand on absorbent kitchen paper to draw out the liquid. Meanwhile, trace the house motifs from this page and transfer them on to thin card to use as templates.

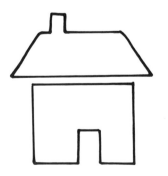

2 Lay the template on to the cut surface of the potato and cut round the edge using the small knife held in a vertical position.

3 Now scoop out the shaded areas, then cut away the excess potato from around the outline to leave the house shape as a raised, flat area.

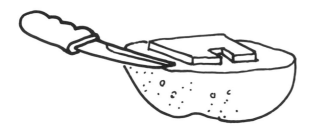

This simple technique can be used to create cards for many other occasions. The pumpkin below, for example, makes wonderful Hallowe'en party invitations. For a firework party use the starburst motif on page 46. Examples of both these cards can be seen on pages 48 and 49.

4 Using the watercolour brush, paint the house area with a generous coating of paint. Then turn the potato over and press it on to clean card. You may get two or three progressively paler printings from each coat of paint. If the potato cut does not print evenly apply a little paint with the tip of the brush while the paint is still wet and blend in the edges. Tiny bare patches do not matter, in fact they add to the charm.

5 Print the house on to the front of a plain mount and then paste the address details inside. Alternatively, print the address on to paper which can then be mounted on to a postcard. Print a house at each top corner to decorate.

Anna Stone

has moved to

Brunel House, Forde Road, Newton Abbot, Devon TQ12 4PU

LINO CUTS

Lino cutting is an old and easy craft to master. Transfer your chosen design to the surface of the lino and cut out with the cutting tools. Remember that the areas that you want to stay white are the areas you cut away, and the remaining flat areas of lino will have the ink rolled on to them and will print on to the card. You can create flat printed areas or make textures and shading by using different cutting techniques.

Summer Party Invitations

A luscious strawberry makes an excellent motif for a summer garden party invitation, or if you prefer draw out your own shapes to make up your own design.

MATERIALS
Small piece of lino
Carbon paper
Lino cutting tools
Rubber rollers
Block printing ink
Paper and card
A small piece of glass to roll out the inks

1 Trace off the strawberry design below and use carbon paper to transfer it to the centre of a small piece of lino.

2 Use the cutting tools to cut away the background areas of the lino to leave the strawberry as a raised area for printing. Cut round the outline first with a narrow cutter and then use a wider cutter to remove larger areas from the rest of the background. Lastly, use a very small cutter to cut out the tiny seeds from the surface of the strawberry.

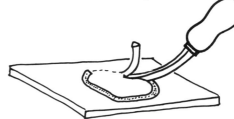

3 Apply a little of the ink to the sheet of glass and use the roller to disperse the ink evenly over the surface of the roller. Run the inked roller over the surface of the lino cut several times until the surface is evenly coated with ink.

4 Lay your paper or card over the lino and use a clean roller to roll over the back of the paper to make the print. Peel the paper off carefully and leave the print to dry. Ink up the lino in the same way for each subsequent print. You may need to practise on scrap paper to get just the right amount of ink and pressure.

5 When the prints are dry, score and fold the cards to make up the invitations as for the stencilled wedding cards on page 57.

To position the lino cut accurately on your cards, lay strips of masking tape on your work surface marking the position of the lino. This will ensure you place it accurately each time you print. Next try a test print. When you are happy with the position of the printed motif, cut the card to the right size and position it back on the lino as if making an identical print. Mark the edges with tape as a guide for further prints.

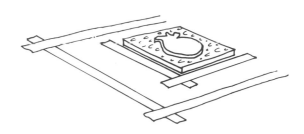

Use the strawberry design to print menu cards and place markers as well as invitations

STAMPED AND EMBOSSED CARDS

Using a stamping and embossing technique is the ideal way of making a quantity of cards and gives a very professional result. You can either use a greetings message stamp, or for a more luxurious look make a white lining sheet to fit inside.

Embossed Cards

Choose a stamp design from the wide range available. Embossed cards, such as the two designs pictured on the top left-hand shelf in the photograph on pages 46–47, look sophisticated and could be used for any number of occasions.

MATERIALS
Thin card in colours of your choice
Coloured ink backgrounds
Fine gold felt-tipped pens
Rubber stamps
Embossing ink
Stamp pad
Embossing powder

1 Roughly cut out pieces of thin card; your measurements need not be accurate at this stage. Squeeze some embossing ink on to the surface of the dry stamp pad. Spread it evenly and then close the lid and allow the ink to sink into the fabric surface for about 15 minutes.

2 Press the decorative rubber face on to the surface of the pad for an even layer of ink. Press the stamp firmly on to one of the pieces of card. Lift off carefully to avoid smudging.

3 Sprinkle embossing powder liberally on to the stamped area and tap the edge of the card to distribute it evenly. Shake the excess powder off on to scrap paper. This can then be returned to the jar for further use.

4 Hold the stamped card very carefully near a heat source such as a hotplate or special heat gun, until the powder melts and goes shiny. This gives an attractive and permanent embossed finish. Do not allow it to overheat but make sure the design is melted all over or it could brush off.

5 Trim the motif and glue onto a plain mount. Add a border with a gold felt-tipped pen.

Stamped Cards

These cards are quick and simple to make, perfect if you have a large circle of family or friends. Add as much extra decoration as you like to personalise each one.

MATERIALS
Rubber or sponge stamps
Sponge roller
Stamping ink
Coloured card and fabric

1 Pour a little of the stamping ink on to an old plate then coat the roller evenly. Cover the surface of the stamp with ink, by rolling back and forth. Do not press hard on the roller or too much ink will be deposited on the stamp, filling up the indentations, and the resulting printed design will not be clear.

2 Practise on different scrap surfaces until you are confident and can apply just the right amount of ink. Then, to print the design, press the stamp firmly against your chosen card or paper. You will need to re-coat the stamp for each impression. Work on small pieces of paper or card and then cut out or use the hand-torn edge technique (see page 11) to mount these on to the main card mount.

3 To position your stamps accurately on a ready cut card, use small pencil marks or strips of masking tape to line up with the wooden edge of the stamp block.

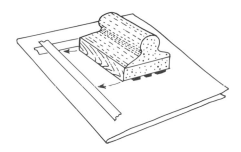

Commercially-available rubber stamps can be used to make attractively-designed cards, such as these two, quickly and in large numbers

Subtle silver and white are always right for weddings and these elegant urns look particularly fine in pairs – one each for the bride and groom. Narrow silver ribbon adds the finishing touch

STENCILLED CARDS

The stencil is made on an acetate sheet, taped to the card, and painted over with fast-drying paints. Stencils can be applied to all kinds of surfaces. Simple shapes work best as every part of the design needs to be held in place by bridges in the acetate sheet.

Wedding Stationery

Weddings can be so expensive but this is the time when everyone wants the day to be perfect. A classic stencil like this elegant urn will look just right printed on to silver or white card for invitations, place names, menus and covers for the order of service in church.

MATERIALS
Acetate stencil sheet
Fine black waterproof felt-tipped pen
Fast-drying stencil paints in white and grey or silver
Small stencil brushes
Silver or white card

1 Tape a piece of stencil acetate over the template on this page. Trace the urn design, using the felt-tipped pen, on to the acetate.

2 Using a craft knife and cutting mat, carefully cut the stencil. Be careful not to cut from one area to the next or you will weaken the stencil and the design will be spoiled. If you do accidentally cut one of the bridges, cover it with masking tape and cut out the areas again.

3 For the invitations, cut out silver or white card 30 x 18cm (12 x 7in). Score two lines 7.5cm (3in) from and parallel to the short sides. Fold these over to make the front of the card.

4 Tape the stencil in place on one side of the card front and paint all over in white, if using silver card. Leave to dry for a few moments and then use a clean brush to add shading here and there in grey. Repeat the stencilling on the other side of the card front. If you are using white card, stencil the two urns in silver.

5 Make up other cards, place names and menus in the same way.

To use the urn stencil for other occasions print it in shades of terracotta and glue on flowers and a butterfly.

The technique of mono-printing is easy to master, and even the youngest member of the family could try their hand at drawing a simple motif, such as a sun or holly leaf

Birth Announcement

You can make these cards (pictured on page 48) before the big event; just add a bow in the appropriate colour and fill in the details. Or wait until the baby has arrived and design it with him or her in mind. The baby's name, weight and birthday can be hand-written with coloured, gold or silver felt-tipped pens or printed.

following the outlines carefully. Tape the stencil to white, pink or blue card and use a small natural sponge to apply the paint. Dab it on lightly to make a soft dappled texture. Try flesh-coloured paint on white card or white paint on the pink or blue card.

MATERIALS
Acetate stencil sheet
Fine black waterproof felt-tipped pen
Fast drying stencil paints in white or peach
Small natural sponge
Pink blue or white card
Narrow ribbons

1 Tape a piece of stencil acetate over the footprint shown. Trace off and cut the stencil

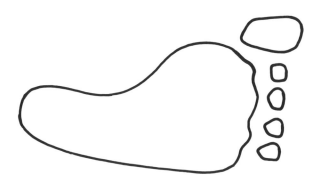

ONE-OFF PRINTING

If you like the printed image but you don't need to make lots of cards, try the following easy one-off technique – mono printing. It involves simple free hand drawing on to the back of paper that has been laid over a piece of glass rolled with a thin layer of ink.

Mono-prints

Choose simple shapes to draw for mono-printing. You can create several similar designs – yet they all will be different as they are hand drawn.

MATERIALS
Block printing ink
Small sheet of glass
Rubber roller
White paper
White spirit
Coloured card
Coloured, gold and silver felt-tipped pens

1 Put some of the printing ink on to a sheet of glass and use the rubber roller to spread it out evenly to a rectangular shape. The ink should form quite a thin layer so that you can still see the glass through it slightly.

2 Very lightly lay the paper face down on to the ink. Now draw on your design using a ballpoint pen or a sharp pencil. Take care that your hand does not rest on the paper as you draw or you will spoil the print.

3 When the drawing is complete lift the paper off carefully and leave the print in a warm place to dry. Make sure the ink is quite dry before you make the print into a card or you may smudge the design.

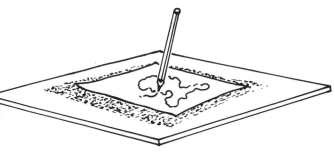

4 For a decorative effect, cut around the edge of your monoprint with pinking shears. You could also colour in areas of your drawn design with felt-tipped pens. Use spray adhesive to glue your decorated monoprint to the front of a folded piece of card.

If you are a bit shaky about free-hand drawing you can draw your mono-print design on the back of the paper first, then go over these lines to make the finished print. Children's drawings look particularly good printed in this way as their naive quality is fresh and charming.

CHAPTER 5

Hand-sewn Cards

*M*aking a hand-sewn card requires special care which is bound to be appreciated by the recipient. The variety of sewing and embroidery techniques include cross stitch, needlepoint, silk ribbon embroidery and patchwork, and will give both the experienced stitcher and those new to the delights of needlecraft something to try their hand at. All the following projects use sewing skills which are easily mastered and can give really impressive results.

The wide variety of sewing techniques described in this chapter can be used to create the range of exquisite cards displayed here

SILK RIBBON EMBROIDERY

Embroidering with fine silk ribbon is a beautiful embroidery technique. As the ribbon is wider than thread, the embroidery develops much more quickly. A simple design, such as a single rose, takes only a few minutes to complete and so is perfect for a last minute card.

Basic Techniques

Once you have mastered the general techniques and familiarised yourself with the particular stitches you will be ready to begin the silk ribbon embroidery projects featured on pages 64-67. Gather together the few simple materials required and practise on a test piece of your own before beginning one of the designs provided.

MATERIALS
Open weave linen or cross-stitch embroidery fabric in the colour of your choice
Silk ribbons in widths and colours of your choice
Needles – chenille size 18 or crewel size 8
Soluble embroidery marker pen

1 In order to thread and secure the ribbon cut it at an angle to make a point. Thread the point through the eye of the needle and pull it through a little way. Push the point of the needle back into the ribbon and push this up towards the eye to make a loop.

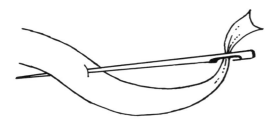

2 Pull the short free end of the ribbon through the eye to eliminate the loop. Then hold both ends of the ribbon together behind the needle so that the eye of the needle is covered and the

ribbon is securely held. This helps the ribbon to pass through the fabric easily and prevents it slipping off the needle whilst you are stitching.

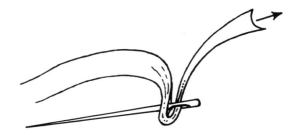

3 Keep the stitch tension fairly loose and even when working with silk ribbon. This allows the ribbon to form the petals in a natural way and still retain a three-dimensional effect. The wider the ribbon the looser the tension should be.

4 To stop the stitches twisting, hold the ribbon down on the right side of the fabric as you make a stitch and pull it through to the back, taking any twists through to the wrong side.

5 To finish, sew down the ends on the wrong side of the work using a fine needle and thread.

6 The tension and different widths of ribbon that you use for each stitch will give totally different results. It is worth experimenting on small pieces of fabric before starting a larger design so that you know what the finished results will be. These experimental pieces can also be made into delightful small cards with the use of decorated window mounts.

7 Mark out your designs on the fabric using a soluble embroidery marker pen. This leaves a faint blue line to guide your stitches. Any marks still showing after stitching can be removed by dipping a watercolour brush in clean water and going over the lines until they have disappeared.

These are the basic stitches you will need to complete the projects on the following pages.

Ribbon stitch

Bring the ribbon up through the fabric, hold it flat and insert the point of the needle back into the fabric through the centre of the ribbon. Pull gently to make a softly curled petal in one stitch.

Stem stitch

Work with a forward and backward movement keeping the stitches the same size and the thread to the left of the needle as shown.

Zig zag border

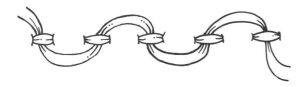

Make a row of well-spaced running stitches in one colour. Weave even-sized loops in and out of the first row using a contrasting coloured ribbon without stitching through the fabric.

Chain stitch

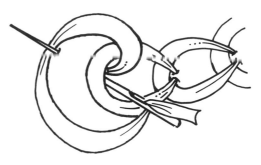

Keep the links of the chain even with regular sized stitches. Do not pull the ribbon tight or the fabric will pucker and the ribbon will be crushed.

Lazy daisy stitch

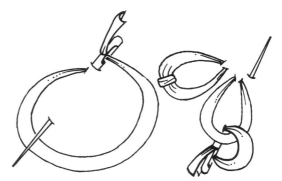

Work as chain stitch but make separate stitches, and hold the loops in place with a small stitch.

French knots

Hold the ribbon taut on the surface of the fabric with the left hand, twisting the needle around it two or three times. Tighten the twists then insert the point back into the fabric and pull the needle through to the back.

Spring Flower Border

The delicate silk ribbon is perfect for representing fresh flower petals. Make up your design using a variety of flowers in different colours.

MATERIALS

Open weave linen or cross-stitch embroidery fabric in the colour of your choice

Silk ribbons in widths and colours of your choice

Needles – chenille size 18 or crewel size 8

Soluble embroidery marker pen

Cards suitable for window mounting

1 Draw a horizontal base line about 8.5cm (3½in) long on to your chosen fabric. Mark the position of the flowers and leaves growing up from the base line. Lightly mark in a border measuring about 10 x 5cm (4 x 2in).

2 Stitch the flowers first (see page 63), using straight stitch and lazy daisy for the daffodils, straight stitch for the tulips, lazy daisy for the crocuses and French knots for the hyacinth.

3 Stitch the stems and leaves for the flowers in straight stitch using narrow ribbons in two shades of green.

4 For the zig zag border, follow the line you have already marked making a row of small, widely spaced running stitches in a narrow ribbon. Using a medium-width ribbon, weave in and out of this row of running stitches to form a two-tone border. Take particular care to keep these stitches flat.

5 Choose a lightly-patterned cream card to make a window mount for this card, cutting an oblong window to fit outside the design. Mount as before using spray glue to enclose the edges of the fabric, as described on pages 11 and 12.

White Briar Rose

The white briar rose on page 66 is set off beautifully against the pale green fabric. Choose your own colours or follow the suggestions given here. Decorate the window with bronze outliner.

MATERIALS

Open weave linen or cross-stitch embroidery fabric in pale green

Silk ribbons in widths and colours of your choice

Needles – chenille size 18 or crewel size 8

Soluble embroidery marker pen

Pebeo bronze relief outliner

Card suitable for window mounting

1 For a white briar rose work on pale green fabric about 10cm (4in) square. Mark the fabric with a centre point and then five equally spaced radiating lines around this, about 2cm (³/₄in) long. Following the stitch diagrams on page 63, make five ribbon stitches following the marked guide lines, using wide white ribbon.

2 Using a narrow pink ribbon, fill the centre of the flower with large and small French knots to complete the design.

3 Trim the fabric to about 3cm (1¼in) from the embroidered area. Tape the embroidery behind a 7.5cm (3in) diameter circular opening in the central panel of a window mount. Make sure the image is centred in the window. Fold over and glue the right-hand panel of card behind the embroidery to enclose the fabric and form the finished greetings card.

4 Decorate around the edge of the window with a simple row of dots made with the bronze relief outliner. Leave to dry before use.

The spring flower border card shows the delicate results to be acheived with silk ribbon embroidery

Cream and Pink Rose

The delicate cream and pink rose (on page 66) has peach-coloured French knots at the centre.

MATERIALS
Open weave linen or cross-stitch fabric in white
Silk ribbons in widths and colours of your choice
Needles – chenille size 18 or crewel size 8
Soluble embroidery marker pen
Card suitable for window mounting

1 Work on a piece of white fabric about 10cm (4in) square. Following the chain stitch diagram, work the centre of the rose in a few small chain stitches to form an oval shape. Use narrow pink ribbon for these stitches and fill in the central space with tiny peach-coloured French knots.

2 Work the outer petals in medium-width, cream-coloured ribbon using a spiral of chain stitches to form the rose shape.

3 Lastly, work a loose lazy daisy stitch in narrow green ribbon to represent each leaf.

4 Choose or make a window mount with an oval window about 6.5cm (2½in) long.

Mauve and Blue Rose

The mauve and blue rose is worked in the same way as the cream and pink rose. A silk ribbon bow is added to this design to make it slightly different.

MATERIALS

Open weave linen or cross-stitch embroidery fabric in the colour of your choice
Silk ribbons in widths and colours of your choice
Needles – chenille size 18 or crewel size 8
Soluble embroidery marker pen
Card suitable for window mounting

1 Mark the rose as before and work the outer layer of petals in blue ribbon stitch, using the wide ribbon. Work on cream or beige fabric about 10cm (4in) square.

2 Work the inner layer of petals in mauve ribbon stitch. Then fill the centre of the flower with French knots made from narrow deep mauve ribbon. Use narrow ribbon in two shades of green, and work in lazy daisy stitch to create the leaves, and then in straight stitch to make some stems.

3 To make the bow, first create the two loops by working large lazy daisy stitches using the wide blue ribbon. Ensure that both loops are the same size. Make a single loose running stitch in the centre to form the knot. Then, carefully bring the ribbon out from the centre of the bow under the knot and cut off the end to make a long tail. Make another tail in the same way and trim them both at an angle to complete.

Blue Daisies

These daisies look stunning stitched in wide blue ribbon with black centres. They are set off to perfection with a deeper blue background.

MATERIALS

Open weave linen or cross-stitch embroidery fabric in blue
Silk ribbons in widths and colours of your choice
Needles – chenille size 18 or crewel size 8
Soluble embroidery marker pen
Card suitable for window mounting

These beautiful silk ribbon embroidered designs can be mounted in a variety of ways. Pictured here are the cream and pink rose (top left); white briar rose (bottom left); mauve and blue rose (top right); and blue daisies (bottom right)

1 Mark the centre points of three daisies and a faint circle around each to make the petals. Then draw in the stems.

2 Stitch the daisy petals in long ribbon stitches using wide blue ribbon. Fill the centre of each flower with carefully placed satin stitch in narrow black ribbon.

3 Work the stems in stem stitch using a narrow shaded green ribbon. Add small side leaves and a blue bud to balance the design.

4 This card was framed in a slightly different way to the others. To complete it carefully glue the embroidery to a piece of backing card. Using a plain mount, cut a window in the front to fit your embroidery. Trim the backed embroidery to fit the card and glue in place behind the window.

CROSS STITCH

Cross stitch is one of the simplest stitches to master, particularly if you work on a special evenweave fabric, such as Aida, which consists of a grid of tiny woven blocks interspersed with holes. To make a cross stitch bring the needle up through a hole in the fabric and make half the stitch by pushing the needle back through a hole diagonally adjacent to the first. Finish the cross stitch by working another diagonal stitch back over the first one. To stitch a row, make a line of diagonal half-stitches and complete them when you stitch the return journey (see diagram below).

Valentine Cross Stitch

This charming little check-bordered cross-stitch heart is quick and easy to make.

MATERIALS
A small piece of white Aida 14-gauge fabric
1 skein of red DMC No 304 stranded embroidery
cotton (floss)
Crewel embroidery needle
Coloured or white card
Checked fabric for the border
Lightweight interfacing

1 Following the chart and stitch diagram on this page, work the heart design in the centre of your fabric. Each square on the chart equals one block of threads on the fabric, and each symbol equals one stitch. Divide the embroidery cotton (floss) and use two strands at a time. Use pieces about 50cm (20in) long to avoid tangling. Try to make all your stitches cross the same way.

2 Before you make the design up into the card, press the embroidery carefully. Lay it face down on to a piece of clean cotton fabric. Lay a similar piece on top and press with a steam iron until it is quite flat.

3 Spray the back of the embroidery with adhesive and then mount it centrally on to the front of a square of folded card.

4 Make a window from check fabric to frame your cross-stitch heart. Iron lightweight interfacing on to the back of the fabric to stop the edges fraying. Mark out the area of the window and cut it out carefully with sharp scissors. Use the checks to help you keep the edges straight. Cut the outer edges of the fabric with pinking shears to fit just inside the edges of the front of the card, and glue it in place with spray adhesive.

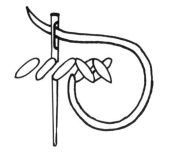

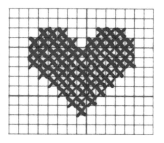

Cross-stitch heart chart

The Valentine cross stitch is pictured here with a pretty padded heart card (see page 44)

Cross Stitch Keepsake

The basket design on the following page makes a pretty card which can be turned into a keepsake.

MATERIALS
A small piece of pale-green Aida 14-gauge fabric
DMC stranded embroidery cotton (floss) as listed in key
Crewel embroidery needle
Coloured or white card
Marbled paper for the mount.
Window mount card (12.5cm/5in square)

1 To stitch the design, carefully follow the chart and key on page 70, referring to step 1 opposite for the basic technique. Then press the embroidery, between two clean pieces of cotton, with a steam iron.

2 Cut a square window in the centre section of your window mount to fit around the outside of the embroidered border. You can cut it to fit exactly, or leave a larger gap all round the edge.

3 Trim the fabric to a 11cm (4¼in) square and tape it centrally behind the window, stretching the fabric evenly. Mask the back and centre section of the card and spray glue on the inside of the front flap. Then fold this in place to enclose the back of the embroidered fabric.

4 To make the decorative border, cut four strips of the toning marbled paper about 1cm (³/8in) wide. Cut the pieces longer than the sides of the window to allow for the mitred corners. Spray the reverse side of the strips with glue and then place them around the window.

5 Using a ruler and craft knife, carefully cut the mitres at the corners going through both thicknesses of paper to make a perfect join (see page 12). Remove the excess pieces of marbled paper and press down the corners firmly to adhere them to the card.

Your cross-stitch card could be slipped into a frame to keep as a memento when the occasion has passed

402   987

721   433

PATCHWORK

This star patchwork technique needs accurate folding but very little sewing and is built up of small squares of fine fabric folded into triangles and arranged in concentric circles to form a star shape. The raw edges are hidden behind a window mount to give a smart, professional finish.

Traditional Patterned Fabric Star

A trio of patterned patchwork fabrics are used to make this beautiful card that could be later framed and turned into a picture.

MATERIALS
Scraps of 3 different patterned fabrics
Scrap of calico for backing
Stiff card template 12cm (4¾in) square
Matching threads
Needle
Fine silver felt-tipped pen
Gold window mount card

1 Decide on the position of the three fabrics in your star design and then cut out the pieces in the following way. Using the card template, draw round and cut out four squares from the central fabric and eight squares from the two remaining fabrics.

2 Fold the squares of fabric exactly in half with right sides outside and press each fold. Bring the folded edges in to meet at the centre thus forming a triangle. Press the folds again.

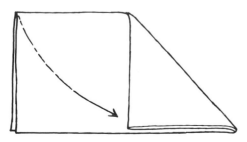

3 Cut the calico to an exact 15cm (6in) square and mark accurately in pencil as shown, to use as a positioning guide.

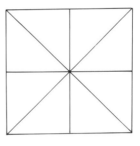

4 Pin the four central triangles in place with the central folds uppermost. Line up the centre folds on each triangle with the diagonal marked lines on the backing fabric and butt them together so that none of the backing fabric shows between them. Make tiny invisible stitches at the centre points of the triangles to secure the fabric to the backing and then tack (baste) all round, close to the raw edges.

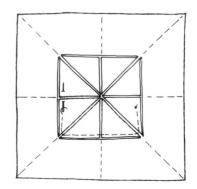

The same patchwork technique is used to different effect with a variety of plain and patterned fabrics. The rich red star is made with a gorgeous assortment of coloured silks embellished with beads, but a delightful traditional look can be gained with patterned patchwork fabrics

5 Take the second row of eight triangles and place each piece on one of the radiating lines. Make sure that all the points are 2cm (7/8in) from the centre. Stitch these triangles at the points to secure them, as before, then tack (baste) all round the raw edges.

6 Position the final row of triangles around the backing fabric as before, leaving about 1.5cm (5/8in) of each triangle showing. Stitch this row of triangles in place.

7 Draw out an octagonal shape to fit round the finished patchwork. Cut out a window to this shape on the central panel of a window mount card. Tape the patchwork centrally behind this and then trim the fabric to fit just inside this. Fold over and glue the right hand panel of card behind it to enclose the fabric.

8 Using the silver felt-tipped pen, draw two parallel lines around the window mount to make a decorative border.

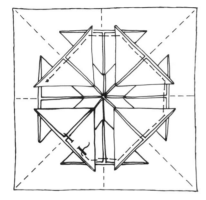

Jewel Coloured Silk Star

This star is made in the same way as the previous project, but uses an assortment of rich coloured silks embellished with beads.

MATERIALS
Small pieces of three different coloured silks
Scrap of calico for backing
Gold seed beads
Four gold bugle beads
Threads to match the bugle beads
Fine needle
Textured gold folded card
Pebeo gold relief outliner

1 Decide on the position of the three different coloured silks then follow the instructions on pages 71–2 to make the patchwork star.

2 Stitch a gold seed bead to the centre of the star and then stitch the four bugle beads around this, following the lines of the patchwork. Attach more gold seed beads to the inverted points of the star to give a little extra sparkle and to add texture to your design. Make sure that you have finished off all the threads at the back of the fabric securely so that the beads do not fall off.

3 Cut an octagonal window in the centre section of your window mount. Mount the star behind the window and use adhesive to glue the front fold over to hide the back of the fabric. Using the gold outliner, draw a wiggly border about 1cm (3/8in) wide all round the edge of the mount.

NEEDLEPOINT

A small needlepoint design can easily be made into an attractive greetings card. Choose from a handful of simple stitches and create a miniature masterpiece.

Basic Stitches

Firstly, cut your wool (yarn) into manageable lengths, about 75cm (30in) is ideal. Choose which of these basic stitches you prefer to work in, and then begin. You could use a combination of all of these stitches to suit the size of the area to be worked.

Half cross-stitch

This stitch is simple and uses the least amount of wool (yarn). However, worked without a frame, it has a tendency to distort the canvas which means that the finished piece must be dampened and reshaped.

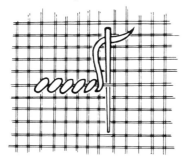

Tent stitch

This uses more wool (yarn) than cross stitch as it makes a longer diagonal on the back of the work.

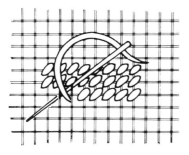

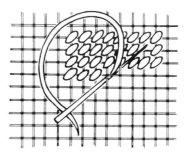

Basket-weave tent stitch

This stitch causes the least distortion of the canvas and is therefore ideal for the larger background areas.

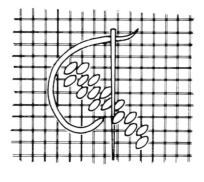

Choose this luscious strawberry design to stitch into a charming card. A summer birthday or anniversary would be the ideal occasion or perhaps you could make it up into a picture or pincushion to send as a gift

Strawberry Sampler

The whole surface area of the canvas is covered in the charming strawberry design shown on the previous page. The colours of wools (yarns) listed below form the key. The stitched area of the design measures about 9.5cm (3¾in) square.

MATERIALS

DMC Tapisserie wools (yarns) – 1 skein of each as follows:

Dark green – No 7428
Mid green – No 7376
Light green – No 7404
Dark red – No 7600
Light red – No 7135
Pink – No 7132
Background colour – Ecru
15cm (6in) square of single thread white canvas (10 holes to 2.5cm (1in))
Size 24 tapestry needle
Stiff card for mount (about 15cm (6in) square)
Folded card

1 Mark the centre of the canvas, both vertically and horizontally with a line of tacking (basting), to match the centre lines on the chart. Count and tack (baste) around the outer edge of the design

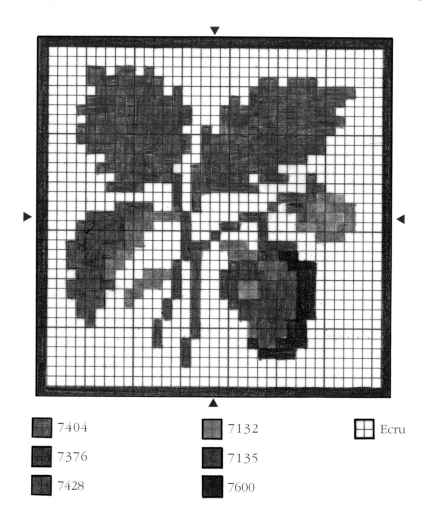

▨ 7404	▨ 7132	⊞ Ecru	
▨ 7376	▨ 7135		
▨ 7428	▨ 7600		

as well. Do not be tempted to mark the canvas with a pencil line as this will rub off on to the wool (yarn) and discolour it. Start stitching in the centre of the design and work out towards the edge, finishing with the background. This is the best way to use a charted design to avoid making mistakes in counting the squares, and remember that each square on the chart represents one stitch on the canvas.

2 Following the chart, stitch the design using the colours in the key. Begin by bringing the wool (yarn) up from the underside of the canvas. Leave about 5cm (2in) of wool (yarn) at the back and hold this in place while you make the first few stitches over it. To finish off, weave the thread behind two or three stitches. You can move to another area of the same colour without fastening off the wool (yarn) but this next area should be no more than 2cm (3/4in) away.

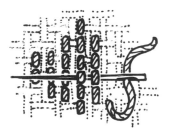

Try to keep the stitch tension regular. You should aim for a smooth even look, so that the wool (yarn) is not so tight that the canvas shows through nor so loose that loops form on the front of the needlepoint.

3 You may need to stretch the canvas after stitching to ensure that it is square for mounting. For this you will need a piece of blockboard, a set square and ruler, a plant spray, several sheets of clean white blotting paper and drawing pins or a staple-gun.

Start by spraying the back of your needlepoint with water so that is very damp but not soaking wet. Lay the sheets of blotting paper out on the blockboard and spray them lightly with water. Place the needlepoint face down on the blotting

paper and pull it into shape with your hands. You may have to pull quite strongly and then check the accuracy with the set square and ruler. Pin or staple along one edge, through the canvas only, stretching it as you go. Now pin the opposite edge, pulling it really taut. Pin the other two sides in the same way, starting at the centre point on each side and working out towards the corners.

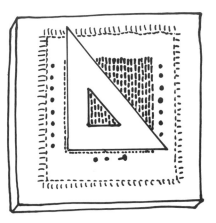

Lightly spray the whole surface of the needlepoint and then leave it in a warm place to dry gently over one or two days. Do not be tempted to dry it too fast against a radiator or you may damage the work.

4 Measure your finished needlepoint and cut a window mount from stiff card to fit exactly round the edge of the stitching. Tape the canvas behind the window and then mount this on to the front of a piece of folded card cut to size.

If you like the design but don't want to stitch it yourself why not assemble all the materials needed and turn it into a tiny kit to send to a friend who loves sewing. You can make a coloured photocopy of the chart and key opposite to send with the materials.

CHAPTER 6

Victorian Cards

❋

*T*he Victorians were fascinated by papercraft and developed so many delightful techniques that it is hard not to look at a delicate découpage collage or intricate quilled card without thinking of this particular period of history. An opulent gold border, or the rich colours of the ribbon weaving card in this chapter are likely to transport you back to an elegant age when decoration was a consuming passion.

These cards are typical of the much-loved Victorian era, and in true Victorian style the more decorative the better

QUILLING

Quilling was a very popular pastime in the Victorian era. Decorative pictures, boxes, tea caddies and even whole cabinets were covered with these tiny spirals of paper, making intricate patterns and floral designs. Sometimes the paper was coloured or even gilded to resemble fine gold filigree work. It is an excellent decorative technique to use for greetings cards today as it is light, surprisingly strong and inexpensive.

Basic Techniques

Before you begin to make up a design, here is the basic method for making quilled shapes.

MATERIALS
White cartridge paper
Quilling tool (or cocktail stick, narrow dowelling or a knitting needle) for rolling the paper strips
Stiff card and coloured paper for mounting

1 Using a craft knife and cutting board, cut the paper into long thin strips about 3mm ($\frac{1}{8}$in) wide. The width of each of these should be accurately cut, so that the surface of the quilling is level when the design is complete. The next stage is to roll the paper into different shaped scrolls. The variation in shape is determined by the length of the paper strip and the way of gluing and pinching the coil before you arrange them into the design. Experiment with a few shapes to get the feel of this craft.

2 Slot the end of the paper strip into the slit in the top of the quilling tool and then wind the paper round firmly, keeping it level. If you glue the end in place now and then remove the paper from the tool, you will have a closed coil that will remain in this shape. These are very useful for filling in areas and making borders. If, however, you remove the paper before gluing, it will unroll slightly and the layers will open out. Glue the end in place at this stage and you have a simple open coil. This is the most usual method for quilling, enabling you to pinch and shape the coil as follows:

Tear drop

Pinch an open coil at one side, after gluing.

When you have mastered all the quilling shapes, make up a few of each and start to lay them out to form patterns. To make regular designs you will need to measure each strip of paper and keep it a constant size, so that all the pieces are the same.

Victorians used the beautiful craft of quilling to decorate all manner of items. Sometimes paper was coloured or even gilded so that it resembled fine gold filigree work. You could use the quilling shapes to create an attractive frame for a small motif or picture

Petal

Make as for the tear drop but curl the pinched end round.

Eye

Pinch the coil at both sides simultaneously.

Leaf

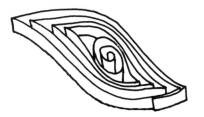

Pinch both sides as for the eye but curl the pinched ends round in opposite directions to make a leaf shape.

Half moon

Press the coil gently round the tool handle and pinch the ends.

Triangle

Fold as for the half moon but pinch the top.

Rectangle or square

Pinch two opposite corners then pinch two more to form either a square or rectangle. This can also be squashed slightly to form a diamond.

Flower Card

Using the basic techniques shown above you can make up the charming flower card which is shown on page 81.

MATERIALS
White cartridge paper
Quilling tool (or cocktail stick, narrow dowelling or a knitting needle) for rolling the paper strips
Stiff card and coloured paper for mounting

1 Make up eight leaf shapes from 30.5cm (12in) long strips of paper. Arrange them in a circle to form a flower, near the top of a piece of blue folded card measuring 15 x 9.5cm (6 x 3³⁄₄in). Lift each piece and spread a little glue on the base of the coil. Replace it at once and then glue the next coil in position. Continue in this way round the flower.

2 Cut four 10cm (4in) strips of paper, and glue them together at one end. Then glue this end between two of the lower petals of the flower. Curve the stem round and glue the other end in place. Make two eye shapes to represent leaves using 30.5cm (12in) strips and glue them either side of the stem.

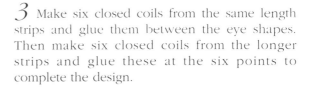

White on White Card

This beautifully patterned quilled card can be seen in the photograph on page 81.

MATERIALS
White cartridge paper
Quilling tool (or cocktail stick, narrow dowelling
or a knitting needle) for rolling the paper strips
Stiff card and coloured paper for mounting

1 Choose a piece of heavy weight watercolour paper and make a folded card measuring 8cm (3¼in) square.

2 Make up six eye shapes from 30.5cm (12in) long strips and glue them in a circle to the centre front of your card.

3 Make six closed coils from the same length strips and glue them between the eye shapes. Then make six closed coils from the longer strips and glue these at the six points to complete the design.

Quilled Frame

When the frame is complete it can be sprayed with a gold metallic paint to resemble fine gold filigree work (see photograph on page 81).

MATERIALS
White cartridge paper
Quilling tool (or cocktail stick, narrow dowelling or a
knitting needle) for rolling the paper strips
Silver or gold spray paint
Stiff card frame

1 Make four open coils from 30.5cm (12in) long strips and glue in place at the corners. Then make an equal number of leaf shapes for each side of the frame using the same length strips. Glue these in place to fill the spaces and then make four closed coils from 15cm (6in) long strips. Glue these shapes at the inside corners to complete.

2 When the glue has dried, colour the whole frame with silver or gold spray paint. Stand the quilling inside an empty cardboard grocery carton, to protect the surrounding area from paint. Spray gently, following the makers instructions, aiming for several light coatings so that the design does not fill in. Then glue on your central motif.

Sometimes it helps to paint a small amount of glue on the sides of the coils as well as the base, to adhere the coils to each other. But be sparing with the glue so that it does not show and spoil the finished effect.

PAPER LACE

Paper doilies and pierced paper decorations make charming Victorian style cards and mounts. The Victorians loved these intricate, lacy cut-outs and they featured extensively in designs for early Christmas cards and invitations. They used to cut and pierce their own designs from paper but nowadays we can adapt ready-cut paper mats to imitate this effect.

Lace-framed Cards

Following the instructions you can recreate a Victorian style card or mount. Experiment by laying your lace design on different coloured backgrounds.

MATERIALS
White paper doilies in different shapes and sizes
Coloured card
Suitable pictures cut from greetings cards, magazines or paper scraps

1 Start by selecting a favourite picture or motif. Then decide whether the subject would look better with the lace decoration as an under- or an overmount. An undermount usually looks best when the picture can be cut out from its background and has an attractive and detailed outline. Sometimes a complete doily will work well as an undermount with very few additions. More often than not, you will need to trim off certain areas of the doily and add pieces here and there to the edge to make just the right shape. Experiment with lots of different pieces, laying out your design on to a coloured background, until you are happy with it.

A charming collection of cards using a variety of paper lace frames. Delicate paper doilies used as under- or overmounts make an intricate frame for these Victorian designs

2 If your design has an undermount, carefully spread or spray glue on to the reverse of the doily and then lay it in place on the card. Position a piece of clean paper over the top and press gently to ensure the doily is attached all over. Do not press too hard or you will flatten some of the original embossing.

3 Next, cut out the picture following the outline and carefully preserve all the detail. Spray glue on to the reverse of this and place it centrally on to the paper lace.

4 For an overmount, lay your picture on a piece of coloured card and experiment by cutting the centre shapes out of several doilies. Lay them on top of the picture to find the best one and trim off pieces that overlap too much.

5 Glue the picture in place first and then the lacy mount. Lastly cut a piece of folded card out to leave a margin round the edge.

Another way to use doilies is to cut out lots of small pieces from different doilies. Glue your picture to white or pale-coloured card and then build up an outer frame from the pieces of doily. Work so that the design is symmetrical and the pieces are evenly spaced.

RIBBON WEAVING

This simple weaving technique is most effective when you use varied widths and colours of satin ribbon. Choose about six different ribbons and glue them in a woven pattern on to thin card before enclosing them inside a blank window mount.

Lustrous Heart

A simple heart shape, circle or diamond makes the ideal window to display ribbons.

MATERIALS
A selection of at least six different satin ribbons
14cm (5^1/$_2$in) square of thin card for backing
16cm (6^1/$_4$in) square of contrasting paper
Window mount card (15 x 45cm (6 x 18in) unfolded)

1 Trace the inner of the two large heart templates on page 126, then transfer this window shape on to the centre of the thin card.

Rich reds and deep pinks are the perfect choice for a sumptuous Valentine heart in the Victorian tradition. Adapt your card for any occasion by designing an appropriately shaped window

2 Cut several 14cm (5½in) long pieces of the ribbons. Spray the backing card lightly with glue and lay strips of ribbon vertically and horizontally, working from the centre outwards. When you are happy with the placing of the central ribbons, lift the ends and weave them under and over each other, pushing the ribbons together so that none of the backing card shows.

3 Work outwards from this in the same way adding and weaving more ribbons until you have covered the marked area. Tape the ends of the ribbon in place with strips of masking tape.

4 Mask the back section of the card and spray glue on to the inside of the centre section and the front flap. Position the ribbon weaving centrally behind the heart-shaped window in the card mount, then fold the front flap in place to enclose the ribbon weaving.

5 To make a border, cut the larger heart shape (page 126) from the square of coloured paper and glue it to the front of the card to make a contrasting mount that fits around the window. Trim any excess paper from round the edge so that the paper is flush with the card.

TARTAN SURROUNDS

Tartan was a very popular Victorian theme for Christmas. The cards on page 88 are made with Victorian cut-outs, small stamped designs, stars and gold motifs which have been cut from doilies. The designs are framed with a wide tartan craft ribbon to give a festive look and to make the most of a simple idea.

Tartan Edged Cards

As well as greetings cards, the small designs could make excellent gift tags with a length of gold cord attached.

MATERIALS
Tartan craft ribbon or giftwrap
Self-adhesive silver and gold stars
Thin card in red, green or white
Fine gold and silver felt-tipped pens
Gold and silver doilies

1 Cut out and fold coloured card to the required size to make your greetings card mount. Cut out four wide strips of tartan giftwrap or craft ribbon to fit each side of the front exactly, leaving a large enough space in the middle of the card for your central design.

2 Spray the reverse side of the strips with glue and lightly place around the edge of the card, level with the outer edges and overlapping at the corners, to form a frame.

3 Using a ruler and craft knife, carefully cut the corners at a 45 degree angle through both thicknesses of tartan simultaneously to make a perfect join (see page 12). Remove the excess pieces at the corners and press the tartan frame in place all round.

4 Use the gold and silver felt-tipped pens to make one or two decorative ruled borders within the tartan frame. Add gold or silver shapes cut from doilies, self-adhesive stars or any stamped or Christmas motifs to make the

central design. You can add a stamped greeting if you wish.

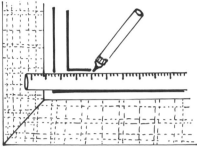

Before cutting out the intricate outer edge of your motifs, cut out any small background areas from the centre of the designs using a craft knife and cutting mat, as the paper will be stronger and less likely to tear at this stage.

5 If you wish, line the inside of the card with white paper (see page 11).

Christmas Stamps

This simple stamping technique, also used to make the attractive star cards pictured on page 55, can be used to create stylish Christmas greetings and gift tags that will be received with pleasure. Many Victorian style stamps are available and are ideal for this type of card.

MATERIALS
Rubber stamps
Roller
Old Plate
Stamping ink
Coloured card and fabric

1 Choose gold, green, red or any Christmas colour for your ink. Coat the stamp evenly with the roller, as described on page 54.

2 Print onto your background by pressing the stamp down firmly. Either cut out the design with pinking shears, or use the hand torn method by following the instructions on page 11. Attach the motif to a plain mount.

3 To position your stamps accurately on a ready-cut card simply follow the instructions given on page 53.

Embossed Greetings

An embossed Christmas message adds a really luxurious quality to these straightforward and easy-to-make cards. The materials are available in sparkling gold and silver, and because the stamps are designed to be used again and again, it is a simple and rewarding task to make enough cards to send to all your family and friends.

MATERIALS
Fine gold and silver felt-tipped pens
Rubber stamps
Embossing ink
Stamp pad
Embossing powder

1 Cut out pieces of background card in various Christmas colours, to the approximate size you will need, ready for stamping. You do not need to be too accurate with your measurements at this stage as you can simply trim the designs to fit your mounts later.

2 Stamp the motif firmly on to the card following the instructions on page 54.

3 Add the embossing powder as described on page 54, and heat it until it melts. Use tongs or pincers, if you have them, to keep your hands at a safe distance from the heat source. Spread the heat evenly under the motif and do not let it over-melt and spoil the design. It is important, however, to make sure that all the embossing powder has melted, otherwise it will brush off.

4 When the embossed pieces of card are ready and the powder has set, cut them out and make them up into cards. You can add decorative borders using gold and silver felt-tipped pens.

ENLARGED ENGRAVINGS

Choose decorative fruit, flower or animal engravings to make these cards inspired by Victorian style. The black and white engravings have been photocopied from a book, enlarged on a photocopier and then hand-coloured with inks and coloured pencils. The designs are then very carefully cut out and mounted on to toning paper.

Fruit Motifs

Attach your chosen motif to the front of a plain card and decorate with borders of gold lines and coloured papers.

MATERIALS
Photocopied motif (from a book out of copyright)
Coloured card
Marbled paper
Fine gold felt-tipped pen

1 Photocopy your motif on to white paper, enlarging it as necessary. Use coloured pencils or inks to colour in the motif in a naturalistic way. Blend the colours and work slightly over the outer edges. There is no need to add shadows as the engraving is already shaded.

2 Cut out the motif very carefully including all the tiny details of leaves, stems and tendrils. Use a craft knife to remove central areas, and scissors around the edge. Spray the reverse side with the adhesive and place centrally on to a piece of toning paper, either plain, marbled or slightly patterned to enhance the print you have chosen.

3 Trim the edge of the paper into a square or rectangle leaving an equal space all round the central motif. Draw on gold border lines with the fine felt-tipped pen if necessary and then glue the design centrally to the front of your folded card.

4 To make a marbled border choose from commercially available marbled paper, cut into strips and mitre the corners as described on page 12. Alternatively, make your own marbled paper by filling a shallow tray with water and floating oil-based inks on the surface. Swirl the inks around a little then lay a piece of high quality paper on the surface momentarily. Lift it off and allow the paper to dry.

These enlarged engravings are very evocative of Victorian-style prints. They could even be individually framed and a group of pictures in this style would make a lovely display in a kitchen or dining room

CHAPTER 7

Modern Art Cards

A variety of different paint effects are used in this section and all with startling and dramatic results. The abstract paintings are great fun and require no artistic expertise as the shapes and textures are quite accidental. The ink-blown effect is stunning and is usually achieved by blowing through a drinking straw. Painting on silk and with watercolours produces particularly delicate finishes and makes wonderful backgrounds.

Brightly coloured inks applied to a variety of surfaces, and delicate watercolours make a exciting range of cards. Use the mounts imaginatively to set off your works of art to great effect. For example, the seascape on the 'bon voyage' card is appropriately seen through the porthole of a ship

ABSTRACT ART

The ink is painted on to stretched watercolour paper and then, whilst it is still wet, creased clingfilm is laid over the top and left to dry. This forms beautiful, random textures and shapes on the surface.

Splashing around with coloured inks is a fun way to make exciting cards. Experiment by adding clingfilm and sprinkling the wet paper with sea salt and gold or silver inks.

MATERIALS
Watercolour or cartridge paper
Drawing board
Sponge
Gummed paper tape
Watercolour brushes
Coloured inks in gold, silver and several colours
Sea salt
Clingfilm
Coloured card to make mounts
Fine felt-tipped pens in gold or silver

1 Begin by stretching the watercolour paper so that it will dry really flat. To do this, cut the paper so that it is slightly smaller than your drawing board. Wet the paper in a large bowl of water for a few moments. Lift it out and hold it up to allow most of the water to drain off. Then place the sheet centrally on to the drawing board and smooth out with the sponge.

2 Tear off four pieces of the gummed paper tape to fit around the edge of the paper.

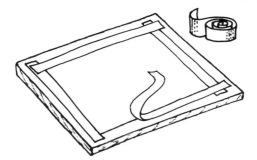

Dampen the back of the tape and paste the tape to anchor the edges of the wet paper to the drawing board. Leave this to dry completely flat in a warm room.

3 Using a large watercolour brush, spread various coloured inks over the surface of the paper. Use some water to merge the colours and let them run into each other in a random way. At this stage you can sprinkle grains of sea salt into the wet ink which will create swirling patterns and concentrated areas of colour. You can also add splashes of gold or silver ink.

4 Whilst the ink is still wet, tear off pieces of clingfilm and let them rest on the surface of the paper. Allow creases to form by gently moving

These attractive cards are achieved with the help of ink, sea salt, clingfilm and a little know-how. Cut out areas of the painted paper to make exciting cards. You can even glue together the left-over pieces, patchwork style, to make a dramatic composition

the clingfilm with your fingertips. When the paper is covered, put the drawing board to one side and leave undisturbed until the ink is completely dry. Do not be tempted to move the clingfilm too soon or the pattern will be spoiled.

5 When completely dry remove all the clingfilm carefully from the surface. Cut the paper off the board using a craft knife.

6 You can use L-shaped strips of card to help you isolate small areas of your designs which make attractive compositions. You may find areas that look like miniature landscapes or even strange animals or flowers. Cut out these areas of the design using a craft knife and ruler.

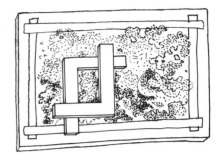

7 To make the cards, spray the reverse side of your cut-out designs with glue and mount them on to card. Choose a suitable colour and add metallic ruled borders drawn with a felt-tipped pen for extra decoration.

INK-BLOWN CARDS

Another technique using a coloured ink background is to place blobs of black ink randomly near the base of your card and then, whilst the ink is still wet, blowing the ink across the surface to create fantastic fairy-tale trees.

Blowing through a drinking straw is the best way to direct the ink and retain some control over the way the trees grow.

MATERIALS
Watercolour paper
Drawing board
Sponges
Gummed paper tape
Watercolour brush
Coloured inks in blue, red, yellow, carmine and black
Drinking straws
Shiny black card to make mounts

1 Stretch the watercolour paper as instructed on page 94. Dip the sponge into clear water and wet the whole sheet of paper so that when you add the coloured inks they will blend together.

2 Then dip the sponge into the ink and spread the colour horizontally across the paper starting at the top. Choose the next colour and apply it in the same way just below the first, using a clean sponge. Continue in this way until the paper is covered and the coloured inks make a background that looks like a vivid sky. Then leave to dry.

3 Using a large brush apply a pool of black ink to the lower area of the paper. Spread this along the bottom edge and add a few more pools of ink to look like tree trunks growing upwards.

4 Now, while the ink is still very wet, blow through a drinking straw towards the pools of ink. Experiment with different strengths of air and by blowing with the tip of the straw at

tree. Add more black ink as you need it and continue blowing until the design is complete.

5 Leave until quite dry and then cut up into interesting shapes for your cards. Using spray glue, mount each piece on to shiny, black folded card for a dramatic effect.

varying distances from the surface of the paper. This action will make the ink spread in little rivulets to look like branches on a silhouetted

These magical ink trees are created by placing black ink randomly near the base of your card and then, while the ink is still wet, blowing the ink across the surface. Use a vivid coloured background for dramatic effect

PAINTED SILK CARDS

Bold and simple designs can be traced through the fine silk on which these cards are painted. The fine lines of gutta separate the paints creating spaces to be flooded with different colours. A variety of effects can be achieved, from stained glass to softly romantic.

Rich-coloured Card

The black outlines and brilliant colours make a bold statement for a man's greetings card.

MATERIALS
Fine black waterproof felt-tipped pen
Fine white silk (about 18cm (7in) square)
Adjustable frame for stretching the silk
Tube of Pebeo gutta in black
Pebeo silk paints in red, yellow and blue
Pebeo thinner
Watercolour paint palette
Watercolour brushes

1 Trace the design carefully from this page using the black felt-tipped pen.

2 Cut out the silk slightly larger than the outer edge of the design. Using the frame, stretch the silk. Tape the design underneath the silk, so that you can see it clearly.

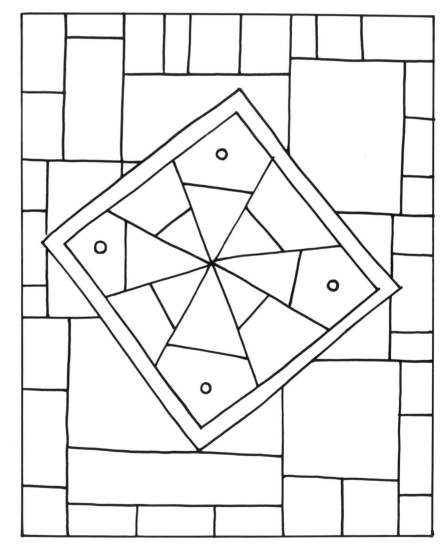

3 Using the tube of gutta with a fine nozzle, draw over the silk following your design lines making sure that all the lines of gutta are solid and joined. If there is a gap, the colours will leak out of one area into the next and spoil the design. Leave the gutta to set for an hour or two before you begin painting.

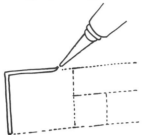

A good way of shading the colour is to dampen the silk with a brush dipped in clean water and then paint the colour on to part of the area only. After a few moments, the edge of this brush stroke of colour will fade gradually to white.

Painting on silk using rich or pale colours has a wonderful effect. The cats painted on silk provide a subtle picture for any cat lover, and the brilliant colours painted into a tracery of black lines makes a strong statement for a man's greeting card suitable for any occasion

4 Mix up the colours for the design in the palette. Try out each shade on scraps of the silk before you paint on the finished article. The colours can be diluted with water or Pebeo thinner for a more pastel effect.

5 To make an even colour, load a watercolour brush with paint and place it lightly on to the silk, in the middle of the appropriate area. Allow the colour to creep up to the gutta outline

gradually, so as not to overload the fabric and possibly bleed into the neighbouring area.

6 If you want to darken any area, put on a few tiny dabs of darker colour in this part, whilst it is still wet. The second coat of colour will slowly seep in and create a subtle shaded effect. To add darker lines or spots, leave the base colour to dry and then use a very fine brush loaded with colour to paint on the details. Paint very lightly so that the lines do not spread.

7 When the whole design is painted, leave it to dry for a few hours in the frame. Remove the next day and fix the silk paints by ironing on the reverse side of the fabric, following the maker's instructions carefully.

8 Tape your finished silk painting inside a window mount card with a rectangular window cut in the centre section. Fold over and glue the end section to neaten the inside of the card.

Pussy Cat Card

This charming design (pictured on page 99) is drawn in outline on to silk with a clear gutta so that the flat areas can be painted in the colours of your choice. When the colours are dry, the gutta is washed out to leave the characteristic delicate white outlines within the design.

MATERIALS
Fine white silk (about 18cm (7in) square)
Pebeo silk paints in pink, grey and green
Pebeo thinner
Tube of Pebeo clear gutta
Watercolour brushes
Watercolour paint palette
Adjustable frame for stretching the silk
Plain white card mount
Fine black waterproof felt-tipped pen
Silver felt-tipped pen

1 Trace the design carefully from the page opposite using the black felt-tipped pen. Follow the instructions for the silk painting project on page 98.

2 Using the tube of clear gutta draw in the main design centrally, and add the swirling background pattern. Leave to set for an hour or two before you begin painting.

3 Mix up the colours in the palette and paint in your design. Paint the cats and heart first and then mix up the background colour with some of the thinner to make a pale wash.

4 When the whole design is painted, leave it to dry then fix the silk paints by ironing on the reverse side of the fabric.

5 Following the manu-facturer's instructions, wash the silk in cool water and rub gently to dissolve the gutta. Roll in a towel to dry and then iron the silk before finally mounting it into card.

6 Tape your finished silk painting inside a window mount with a rectangular window cut in the centre section. Fold over and glue the end section to neaten the inside of the card. Draw a ruled border around the edge of the window using a silver felt-tipped pen.

SIMPLE WATERCOLOUR CARDS

Watercolour painting is quite easy if you follow the simple rule of starting from the top and working downwards. Leave each area of paint to dry before you start the next. Always use a good quality watercolour paper and stretch it before painting.

MATERIALS
Watercolour paper
Drawing board
Gummed paper tape
Small natural sponge
Watercolour paints
Large watercolour brushes
Clean tissues
Coloured card to make mounts
Fine felt-tipped pens in gold and silver

1 Start by stretching a piece of paper slightly smaller than your drawing board as on page 94. Leave until it has dried flat.

2 Using a soft pencil, draw very light lines to create a simple landscape of hills and fields or perhaps a seascape. Use the template on page 102, or use a photograph or magazine cutting to help you compose your design. You can paint one large composition or several small ones on the same sheet and cut them up later to make into your cards.

3 To paint the sky, dip the sponge into clean water and wet the whole of the sky area on your design. Whilst it is still wet, mix up a pale greyish-blue watercolour wash and use a large brush to cover the whole area as quickly as

Make up sheets of different coloured watercolour washes to use as mounts in all your card making. The subtle colours and paper texture give an exclusive hand-made look to your designs.

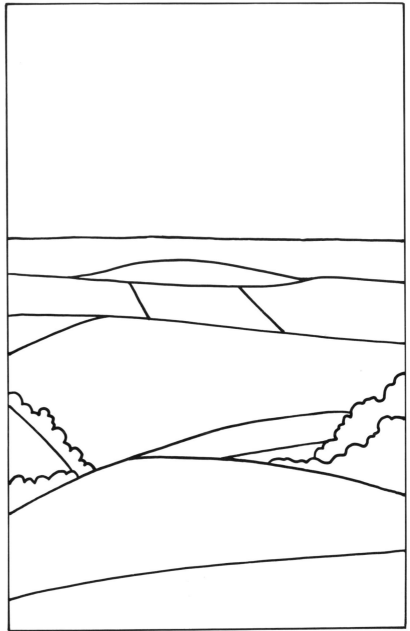

possible. Work from the top of the composition in wide horizontal bands of colour down to the horizon. Don't go back over the paint or you will make unnecessary brush marks but you can add slight changes of colour as you go.

4 Whilst the sky is still wet, make clouds by crumpling a clean paper tissue and dabbing it here and there. This soaks up a little of the paint, and leaves small white areas to represent clouds.

5 Meanwhile, mix up the other colours for your picture. Choose pale bluish-greens for the distance and warmer yellow green shades as you come down the design, towards the foreground. Try out the colours on scrap paper noting that they will dry to a paler shade.

6 Now paint in the hills and fields working from the top of the picture downwards. Leave each area to dry before painting the one touching it, otherwise the paint will bleed and the colours will merge. You can speed up the process by drying small areas with a hair drier.

7 When the whole painting is dry, cut it out around the edges to release it from the board.

You can use L-shaped strips of card to help you isolate small areas of your design which make attractive compositions (see page 96).

8 Choose a coloured card in a suitable shade to compliment your picture, and fold to make a plain mount. Use spray glue to attach your pictures to the front. Using a ruler and fine felt-tipped pen, draw a border around the edge to complete the card. Glue on a tiny bunch of dried or silk flowers for an extra special card.

Bon Voyage

A ship's porthole is an ideal motif to wish someone 'bon voyage'. Paint a watercolour seascape to show through the porthole, as pictured on page 93, and you're ready to set sail.

MATERIALS
Plain blue card mount
Watercolour paper, brushes and paints
Mottled grey paper
Silver felt-tipped pen
Folded paper for lining

1 Use a pair of compasses to draw a circle on the inside of the front flap of your card. Cut this out carefully using a craft knife and cutting mat.

2 Make the watercolour seascape following the instructions on page 101. Simply draw a pencil line for the horizon then paint a sky above,

leave to dry, and then add a slightly darker blue wash below to represent the sea.

3 When the watercolour is dry, cut a piece of it out to fit inside the card, behind the window. Use spray adhesive to mount in on to the lining paper so that it shows through the window.

4 Cut out a ring of mottled grey paper to fit around the window. This could be cut from a watercolour painting or simply a piece of giftwrap. Use the silver pen to decorate this with lines, dots and small circles to represent a ship's porthole and then glue it to the front of the card. Glue the lining into the card to complete.

Small watercolours like these can be cut out of a larger picture or just be a simple wash like a sky with a distant horizon

CHAPTER 8

Collage Cards

*C*ollage is a wonderful way to create abstract designs using small pieces of different materials arranged and glued on to a background. There are three types of collage in the following chapter: natural, using dried or pressed flowers, feathers or shells; paper, using everything from the finest tissue through to corrugated card, cellophane and metallic foils; and fabric, using scraps of shot silks, tiny prints, lace, ribbon, beads and cord.

Making this style of card can be great fun. The skill comes from the choice and arrangement of the various pieces.

Choose printed, patterned, metallic and textured papers which are as varied as possible from the wonderful selection in many art and specialist paper shops. Dry your own flowers or press them, and collect swatches of beautiful fabric, braids, ribbons and lace to create a card from this delightful selection, or to make exciting gift tags

NATURAL COLLAGE

Collecting shells and pressing flowers and leaves is a charming pastime in itself. But carefully arranged on the right background, these natural treasures make exquisite decorated cards, which can bring lasting pleasure to a friend or relative.

Dried Flowers

Choose a warm, dry day to select your flowers and experiment with different varieties.

MATERIALS
Various fresh flowers and leaves
Hot glue gun
Raffia
String
Assorted papers and corrugated card

1 Pick small blooms and sprigs of statice and lavender at the height of their season, choosing a warm, dry day. Select flowers that are not quite in full bloom, as they will continue to develop slightly while they are drying. Experiment with different flowers and you will soon find the perfect moment to pick each type of plant, so that it dries looking its best. Rose buds are a little more flexible, regarding the precise moment of picking. But try to choose ones where the colour of the petals is quite obvious and the green sepals have opened and drawn back. Tiny wild rose buds dry very well and are perfect for a miniature posy.

2 To dry the flowers, strip off most of the leaves and hang them up in small bunches. Tie the stems loosely with string and suspend them near the ceiling of a warm room or in an airing cupboard. The time taken to dry out will vary with different flowers but touch is the best way to tell when they are ready. They should feel quite dry and papery and the stems will be hard and brittle.

3 Cut the flower stems fairly short, and tie them into a tiny flat bunch with a bow made with raffia or ribbon. Choose your backing card and glue the flowers in place with PVA or a hot glue gun. Glue or punch holes and tie your arrangement to the front of the chosen folded card to complete.

If you are sending a card to a friend who's keen on flowers why not choose the flower associated with their birthsign from the list below.

AQUARIUS Orchid, golden rod	**TAURUS** Rose, poppy, foxglove	**LEO** Sunflower, marigold	**SCORPIO** Geranium, rhododendron
		VIRGO Anemone, all small bright-coloured flowers	
PISCES Waterlily	**GEMINI** Lily-of-the-valley		**SAGITTARIUS** Pinks, carnations
ARIES Honeysuckle, thistle	**CANCER** Acanthus, convolvulus, all white flowers	**LIBRA** Large roses, hydrangea and all blue flowers	**CAPRICORN** Pansy, ivy, hemlock and medlar

*Try your dried flowers on a variety of coloured backgrounds until you find just
the right blend of tones, textures and colours*

Pressed Flowers and Leaves

Gather together your selection of flowers, perhaps choosing the favourite blooms of the person you are making the card for, and place them on a sheet of folded blotting paper for pressing.

MATERIALS
Fresh flowers and leaves for pressing
Raffia
String
Assorted papers
Watercolour brushes
A large heavy book or a flower press
Sheets of clean blotting paper
Tweezers

1 Collect the flowers on a dry day after any dew has dried completely. Select several of the same type of blooms, a few buds and some small pieces of foliage. The most successful flowers are ones that grow fairly flat on the plant and so do not become too distorted when pressed. Yellow, mauve and blue flowers keep their colour better than some others, but it is still worth trying pink and red ones, even though they tend to discolour after a while. Colourful autumn leaves can also be used.

2 Carefully cut the flowers from the stems and leaves and lay them out on to a sheet of folded blotting paper. Arrange the blooms on the sheet leaving space for them to flatten out. Press the foliage and stems on another sheet. Fold the blotting paper over to enclose the plants and put them between the leaves of the book. Pile

These collage cards use natural materials such as flowers, leaves, shells, feathers, and all are mounted on a complementary coloured and textured backing sheet

more books on top to weight it down and then leave for about three weeks to dry out. Check after this time, carefully opening the blotting paper so as not to tear the fragile petals. If the flowers are papery and flat and they come away from the blotting paper easily, then they are ready, but they may need another week or two to dry out before you can use them safely.

3 Pick up the flowers with tweezers and move them about with a dry brush. Lay them on to your selected paper background and when you are happy with the design, lift a petal here and there and dab a little glue underneath, to hold it

in position. You can use spray adhesive on the back of petals and leaves for a more secure arrangement or even protect your designs with clear self-adhesive plastic. Add a touch of gold paint applied with a fine brush to subtle coloured flowers like hydrangeas.

4 Try your arrangement mounted on different coloured backgrounds until you find just the right blend of tones, textures and colours. Then use spray adhesive to mount them on to the front of your folded card. Add any drawn border lines at this stage to decorate or tie in a lining paper with a strand of raffia or string.

Sea Shell Card

A selection of beautiful little shells can be collected during a walk on the beach. Try to gather as many as you can if you do not visit the sea shore very often, then you can take shells from your collection whenever you are making a greetings card. Once you have decided on the arrangement of shells attach them with hot glue to a complementary backing card.

MATERIALS
Small shells
Hot glue gun
Raffia
String
Assorted papers and corrugated card
Watercolour brushes

1 Choose a selection of tiny sea shells and arrange them on fairly stiff paper or card. When your design is ready, use a hot glue gun to attach them securely to the backing card.

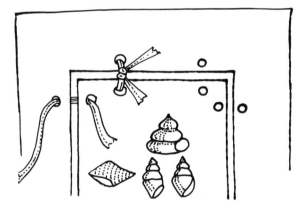

2 For completely natural effect, you can punch holes around the edge of the backing card at each corner and match them up with holes punched around a cut-out window on your folded card mount. Lay the piece of backing card inside the window and then tie it in place using pieces of raffia or coarse string to finish off the card.

PAPER COLLAGE

The wonderful choice of paper is inspiration itself and simply cutting or tearing up pieces to arrange in colourful compositions makes paper collage an easy and enjoyable craft.

Scrap Paper Collage

The cards shown on the following page are ideal for a beginner as you can use pretty scraps left over from other projects. Cut the pieces into shape and simply mount them on to the front of a simple card.

MATERIALS
Scraps of painted backgrounds, giftwrap and card
White card
Pebeo gold and silver relief outliner
Folded card for mounts

1 Using pinking shears or a sharp knife cut the pieces of painted background into small squares and rectangles. Arrange these on to a piece of card or your chosen giftwrap and then glue them in place.

2 Use the outliners to draw on motifs, lines and rows of dots to decorate the pieces. Use spray adhesive to glue the design to the front of folded cards in suitable colours.

Flower Cut Outs

Printed flowers from magazines or giftwrap can be cut out and glued on to pretty backgrounds to make quick cards (see pages 108 and 109).

MATERIALS
Pebeo gold relief outliner
Printed flowers from magazines or giftwrap
Pressed ferns or leaves
Folded card

1 Choose your printed flowers and cut them out carefully using small sharp scissors. Follow the outlines cutting around and including as much detail as possible.

2 Try the flowers on various types of paper and card and choose the one which looks best. Cut out a plain mount from this and use spray adhesive to glue the paper flowers in place.

3 Finish the card with ruled borders or a row of tiny pressed leaves and a raffia tie.

Hand-made and textured papers look particularly good with hand-torn, rather than cut edges. To do this successfully, lightly mark the area with a pencil line and then lay a metal ruler along the inside of the line. Press down firmly with one hand on the ruler and pull the strip of excess paper sharply along the ruler edge to tear it neatly (see page 11). This will leave a slightly uneven edge which follows the texture of the paper. This is perfect for regular shapes but if you want random shaped pieces simply tear by hand and let the paper dictate the shape.

A variety of techniques and finishes are shown here. The quilling is used as a frame to give a Mexican-style effect, the other three collage cards are each different and dramatic in their own way using varied techniques and backgrounds

Modern Quilling

Use the quilling technique (see pages 80 and 81) to make a Mexican style frame for a modern looking card with a sun motif.

MATERIALS
White watercolour paper
White cartridge paper
Scraps of giftwrap
Pebeo gold relief outline
Thick coloured card

1 Cut out a 10cm (4in) square of white watercolour paper. Following the quilling instructions on page 82 make up sixteen square shapes from 30.5cm (12in) long strips.

2 Glue four quilled square shapes at the corners of the watercolour paper. Glue another four squares at the centre point of each side of the paper and then squash the remaining quilled squares into diamond shapes to fit into the gaps. Glue these in place to complete the quilled frame.

3 Choose a motif from giftwrap or another source and glue this inside the quilled frame. Decorate with gold outliner pen and glue the whole piece to a square of toning card. Cut another piece of the same card to this size for the back.

4 Place the pieces of card together with right sides outside and punch five equally spaced holes down the left hand side. Carefully measure where you want the holes before you start. Tie the cards together with pieces of narrow gold braid threaded through the holes. You can also include two lining sheets at the same time.

Natural Torn-paper Collage

Natural-coloured paper hand torn into random shapes and arranged artistically on a textured background looks particularly effective.

MATERIALS
Scraps of various hand made papers, giftwrap, tissue and card
Corrugated paper
Pebeo gold relief outliner
Piece of cord

1 Tear about five pieces of hand-made and natural-coloured paper into random shaped pieces. Arrange these on to corrugated card to form a good composition and use the spray adhesive to glue them in place. Choose a small motif like a sun or flower from giftwrap or another source and glue this in position.

2 Use the gold outliner to draw tendrils, stars, lines, dots and borders to decorate your composition. Trim the corrugated card so that your design is placed slightly to the right of the piece. Cut another piece to the same size for the back of the card. Place them together and punch two holes down the left hand side.

3 Cut out two small squares of darker corrugated card and two small circles of patterned paper. Punch a hole in the centre of each to make decorative washers. Using a piece of cord, thread the back and the front of the card together so that the ends of the cord are at the front. Thread on the square then the round washer and knot both ends of the cord.

Paper Magic

These fun cards, pictured below, are a fast and simple way to send details of baby's birth. Tear thin paper into simple shapes to make up the design of your choice. Position on a plain card mount.

MATERIALS
Thin paper coloured on one side
Thin coloured card
White paper

1 Draw out your shapes very lightly in pencil on to the coloured paper. Tear the paper to make the shape you have drawn, leaving a random white border all round the edge. Choose different coloured paper for each component of the design.

2 Using spray adhesive, glue the shapes, overlapping each other, on to the front of the folded cards.

3 Make linings of white paper slightly smaller than the cards. Then, either hand write the baby's details or greeting on each one, or photocopy your message from a master copy.

Using thin paper in several different colours, tear out the required shapes to make up a composite picture. Mount on brightly coloured card for a fun finish

FABRIC COLLAGE

Carefully chosen, arranged and mounted, even the tiniest scraps of precious material can make a greetings card to treasure. Fray out the edges into a luxurious fringe, add beads, braids and stitchery and you have a tiny work of art in fabric.

Baby Bootee

Use a pretty baby's bootee card to make a birth announcement or as a birth congratulations card. You could make the card up in the appropriate pink or blue, if you choose.

MATERIALS
Scraps of braid, lace, cord and ribbons in pastel colours
Pink or blue card

1 Score and fold a 12.5x 25cm (5 x 10in) piece of pink or blue card in half across the width. Using the template on page 127 trace off the bootee shape and place the dotted line against the folded edge of the card. Draw round and cut out the bootee shape.

2 Use scraps of lace, ribbon and braid to decorate the front of the bootee card. Cut the pieces roughly to length, glue in place then trim level with the edge of the card using scissors.

3 Take a piece of pink or blue cord and dip the ends into PVA glue to prevent untwisting and then tie into a bow. Glue the bow to the front of the bootee.

Silk Mosaic

Arrange and glue tiny swatches of shot silk into a colourful fabric mosaic.

MATERIALS
A selection of scraps of shot silk
Gold-patterned paper
Folded card

1 Cut a selection of vivid coloured shot silks into small squares and rectangles. Fray the sides of each to make fringed edges and then arrange them on to a piece of gold-patterned paper.

2 When you are happy with the composition pick up each piece (you may find it easier to use tweezers to do this), spray the reverse side with adhesive and press in place on to the card to build up the design. Cut the paper into a rectangle with pinking shears leaving enough room to allow space around the fabric pieces.

3 Mount this design on to the front of a plain mount in a suitable colour to complete your greetings card. Trim the edges of the card to leave an equal border all round.

Provençal-print Diamond Card

All the brilliance of a day in the south of France is captured in the bright Provençal prints used in this simple patchwork diamond.

MATERIALS
Scraps of four different Provençal prints
Blue patterned window mount

1 Cut the fabric scraps into 10 x 7cm (4 x 2¾in) rectangles. Stitch one blue and one yellow piece together along the long sides and with right sides together. Press the seam open on the reverse and then stitch the other two together in the same way but this time reverse colours.

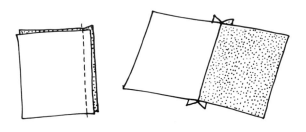

2 Lay the two joined pieces together, right sides together and line up the centre seams exactly. Stitch these together and press the seams as before.

3 Cut a diamond-shaped window in the centre section of the card using the template on page 126.

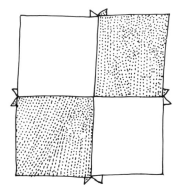

4 Tape the fabric patchwork behind the diamond window and fold over and glue the front flap in place to hide the back of the fabric.

Oriental Carpet Card

A small square of vivid red silk with beads, lace and gold outliner make a card that looks like a rich eastern carpet.

MATERIALS
Scrap of red silk
Scrap of dark papery lace
Beads
Pebeo gold outliner
Piece of gold textured card
Plain silver card mount

1 Fray a piece of red silk as for the mosaic card on page 115, and mount this on to a piece of papery blue lace using spray adhesive. Mount both of these on to a piece of textured gold card and trim the gold card to make a narrow border around the edge.

2 Mount the fabric collage on to the front of the silver folded card. Using the gold outliner, draw a zig zag line down each side of the red silk. Add dots between the points and while the outliner is still wet press on some small turquoise beads. Make a diamond shape in the centre and larger dots of outliner at the corners. Press more small and large beads in place to decorate.

Here are a variety of ways in which you can use fabric in a collage. Using completely different fabrics produces an array of gorgeous cards: a Provençal-print diamond, a silk mosaic and a beautiful beaded oriental carpet

CHAPTER 9

Novelty Cards

A novelty card can double as a gift
and makes the perfect greeting for
any member of the family from the
puzzle fanatic to the sports fan. You
could even delight a sweet-toothed friend
with an edible card. From pop-up cats to
a birthday cake card, the following fun
ideas are easily adapted to suit.

*A selection of novel ideas for novelty cards. With
careful packing a variety of unusual greetings
can be sent through the post*

EDIBLE CARDS

These cards look good enough to eat! Made from edible sheets of rice paper and decorated with food colouring pens, they could also be used as party place settings.

MATERIALS
Sheets of white rice paper
Food colouring felt-tipped pens
Ready-made cake decorations
Flying saucer sweets
Watercolour brush
Pieces of narrow ribbon
Icing sugar
Black felt-tipped pen

> *Rice paper is quite brittle and so the cards are best if made up with an outer and an inner sheet to give them strength. The thin sheets are quite translucent so you can trace through them.*

Owl Card

1 Carefully fold a sheet of rice paper in half without splitting it. To do this draw a faint pencil line where the fold should be. Dip the watercolour brush in clean water and paint a thin line along the pencil line. Whilst this line is still damp fold it carefully so that it does not crack. Leave it to dry under a book.

2 Take a piece of tracing paper at least twice the size of the half-owl pattern. Fold the paper in half and, placing the fold on the dotted line, trace off the pattern. Turn the paper over and trace in the other half to make the complete shape. Slip the tracing inside the folded rice paper card and, following the shape through the paper, draw the owl on the outside of the card.

3 Choose two green flying saucer sweets and draw eyes on them. Using the icing, 'glue' the two sweets in place for the owl's eyes. To do this but keep the card edible, mix some icing sugar to a thick paste with a little beaten egg white. Apply this with the tip of a small knife to the back of the decoration and then press it on to the rice paper card. Leave to dry flat.

4 Make up a lining, on which to write your message, using a second piece of rice paper and slip it inside.

Flower Card

1 To make the edging on the larger card cut the edge of the outer sheet of rice paper with pinking shears. Then colour in the points of the zig zags with the food colouring pens to make a decorative border.

2 Draw on the basket, flower stems and inner border. Use icing to stick the flowers and leaves in place. Draw on the lettering using a tracing underneath to guide you. Slip the lining piece inside each card and tie the layers together with a piece of narrow ribbon finished with a bow.

Children, or indeed anyone with a sweet tooth, will enjoy these edible rice paper cards

BIRTHDAY SURPRISES

A selection of delightfully unusual card designs for fun lovers everywhere, each of these cards has a built-in surprise.

Birthday Cake Card

Send a cake card with real candles to celebrate a birthday. You can glue on the right number of candles – if there's room!

MATERIALS
Silver cake frill
Gold cake candles
Coloured plain mount
Scraps of hologram paper

1 Cover a 10 x 7cm (4 x 2¾in) piece of card with patterned paper, and glue a strip of cake frill across the centre. Cut the long top and bottom edges of the card with pinking shears.

2 Attach sticky tape to the short ends on the wrong side. Fold the tape back on itself and press

to the front of the mount so it curves away from the surface to look like a cake.

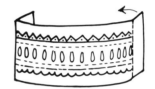

3 Glue the cake candles to the card across the top of the cake. Tuck the base of each candle just below the top edge of the strip of card.

4 Cut flame shapes from hologram paper and glue them on to the card behind each wick. Send the card in a padded envelope to protect it.

Training Shoe Card

Send this fun card to a sports fan or to a small child who's learning to tie laces.

MATERIALS
Shiny and matt black card
Silver felt-tipped pen
White card
Scraps of patterned paper
Scrap of hologram paper
Shoe lace

1 Trace the shoe template from page 127. Transfer the outline on to the front of a plain mount made with matt black card, lining up the dotted lines with the folded edge. Cut the shape out and draw in the inner sole with a silver line.

2 Using the tracing, transfer and cut out the white, patterned and shiny black parts of the design. Glue the zig zag shape and the lower end of the tongue in place.

3 Glue the patterned pieces on to the sides of the shoe, then punch the holes. Use the silver pen to draw on the stitching and to colour around the holes. Insert the shoe lace (being careful not to smudge the silver) and tie a bow. Spread glue around the edges of the reverse side of the shoe upper and press it on to the mount.

4 Now glue on the heel support and the toe cap. Finally, draw on the remaining lines of stitching in silver, to finish the design.

Pop-up Card

The friendly black cat on page 118 is just waiting to bring good luck to the person receiving this card.

MATERIALS
Silver card
Matt-black card
Scraps of hologram card
Small piece of raffia
Scrap of white card
Silver felt-tipped pen

1 Cut a piece of the silver card 11.5 x 33cm (4¹/₂ x 13in). Score across the width on the reverse side and fold so the silver is on the inside.

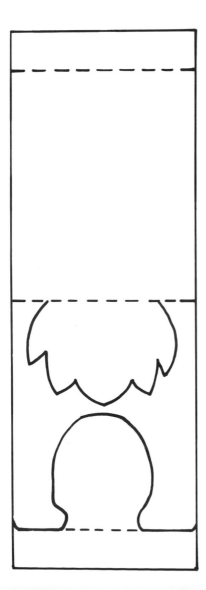

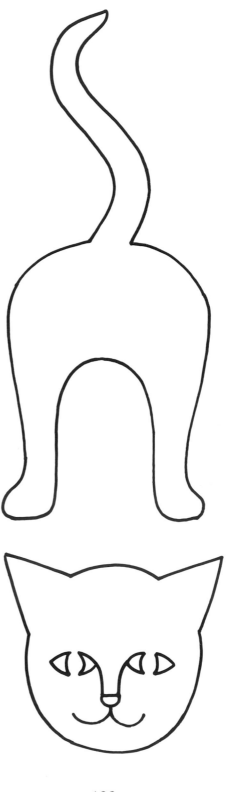

2 Trace off the shapes on the previous page. Cut out the stand from silver card and the cat's body, head, front and back legs from black card, and the chest from white card.

3 Glue the back legs centrally to the inside of the card so that the feet touch the inside fold.

Write your message on the reverse of the jigsaw card so that it can be read when the picture is assembled. For the pop-up card you could adapt the pattern to make all sorts of animals

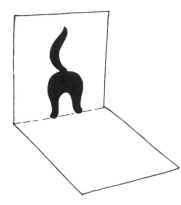

4 Glue the front legs to the stand and score along the dotted lines to make tabs. Fold these tabs under and spread with glue. Fold the stand

in half along the central dotted line and place the piece inside the card, lining up the back of the body with the back legs so that the cat will stand up when the card is opened. Press the tabs firmly to glue securely.

5 Glue the white chest piece in place. Draw the cat's features in silver and glue on the eyes. Cut two pieces of raffia and glue on to the cat's face. Shred the ends of the raffia to make whiskers. Glue the head on to the body.

Jigsaw Card

If you know someone who's always wanted a sports car this jigsaw may be the only way to grant their wish.

MATERIALS
Picture to use as jigsaw
Felt-tipped pen
Piece of thick white card
Fine sandpaper
Thin card to make box
Double sided tape
Small picture of finished jigsaw

1 Cut out the picture, spray the reverse with glue and press it on to the thick white card. Let the glue dry, then trim the edge to make a rectangle. Write your message on the reverse.

2 Draw the shape of the jigsaw pieces on to a piece of tracing paper the same size as your picture. Transfer the lines on to the picture and cut out with a craft knife and cutting mat.

3 Using sandpaper, smooth off any rough edges. Roll the sandpaper into a narrow tube to sand the curved slots slightly so they fit well.

4 For the base of the box, follow the diagram and draw out the shape on to red card. Cut it out along the solid lines and score along the dotted lines on the right side of the card. Bend the card along the scored lines to form the sides

of the box base. Fold in the square pieces at each corner and stick them in place with double-sided tape.

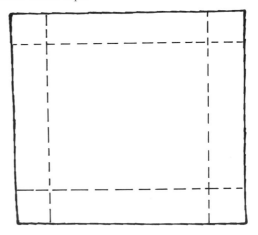

5 Make up the lid in the same way but cut it slightly larger to allow it to slip over the base. Glue a small picture of the completed jigsaw on to the centre of the lid to complete.

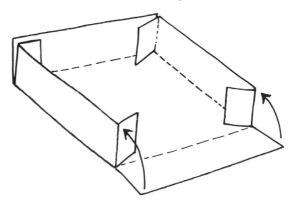

Templates